THE
POWER OF PENTECOST,
THE
POWER IN HANDS

JOE L. CARUANA, MBE, GMD

AuthorHouse™ UK
1663 Liberty Drive
Bloomington, IN 47403 USA
www.authorhouse.co.uk
UK TFN: 0800 0148641 (Toll Free inside the UK)
UK Local: 02036 956322 (+44 20 3695 6322 from outside the UK)

Because of the dynamic nature of the Internet, any web addresses or links contained in this book may have changed since publication and may no longer be valid. The views expressed in this work are solely those of the author and do not necessarily reflect the views of the publisher, and the publisher hereby disclaims any responsibility for them.

Any people depicted in stock imagery provided by Getty Images are models, and such images are being used for illustrative purposes only.
Certain stock imagery © Getty Images.

All Bible quotations have been taken from the New American Bible (NAB; 1970). I used Strong's Online Concordance when researching a Bible location or confirmation of a text.

This book is printed on acid-free paper.

ISBN: 978-1-6655-9628-2 (sc)
ISBN: 978-1-6655-9627-5 (e)

Print information available on the last page.

Published by AuthorHouse 02/02/2022

ACKNOWLEDGEMENTS

I wish to thank Father John Pardo, Vicar General of the Diocese of Gibraltar and former rector of the Royal and Pontifical English College of St Albans in Valladolid, who was appointed Chancellor and judicial Vicar by the late Bishop Caruana for his invaluable help as he read the manuscript of this book and made some very helpful technical corrections at a time when he was pressed by many other duties.

He gave me a list of notes with corrections and suggestions. Among his notes he made the following comment:

> Well done, if I may say! I enjoyed reading your testimonies. It saddens me that in the measure historically Catholic countries succumb to secularisation; faith in the Real Presence also suffers. I see initiatives such as your book as an opportunity to reinforce the truth and evangelise.

I would also like to thank Mr Anthelmo Torres of Fotografiks Designs for scanning and improving the photos in the book.

CONTENTS

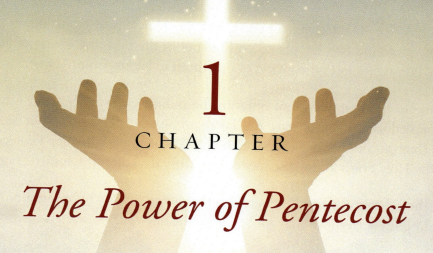

The Power of Pentecost

The Power of Pentecost, the Power in Hands was written in 1984, when I lived in Calgary, Canada, and I was heavily involved in my industrial diamond business.

After returning to my Church, in 1983, I felt a powerful drive to get involved in the affairs of my Parish church, St Bonaventure Church at Parkland Drive, there I enrolled to take religious studies at the Diocesan Centre in Calgary.

The Jewish Shavout.

Pentecost" is a Greek word that means fiftieth. Was this important? Well yes because in the Old Testament, the Feast of Pentecost is also called the Shavuot, which falls fifty days after Passover. It is also known as the Feast of Harvest (Exod. 23:6; Lev. 23:15–16), the Feast of Weeks (Exod. 34:22), and the Day of First Fruits (Num. 28:26).

To understand Pentecost, we must see it against the background of Shavuot, one of the three biblical pilgrimage festivals and known as the "Pentecost". This festival marks the completion of the seven-week, or fifty days, between Passover and Shavuot.

It was not a coincidence that Heaven opened and the Holy Spirit came down on Jesus' disciples. Something equally profound had happened on Shavuot in the past, the giving of the Torah. In Jewish tradition, Shavuot commemorates the giving of the Torah to Moses from 'Above'.

The Israelites came to the foot of Mount Sinai in the month of Sivan. Since it was also the month of Shavuot, the rabbis deduced that God gave the Torah on Shavuot. Thus, Shavuot became the Festival of the Giving of the Torah at Mount Sinai (Exod. 12:6–12). And the new Christian Pentecost was the occasion of the Giving of the Holy Spirit to the disciples of Jesus fifty days after the resurrection of Jesus Christ.

We can now see these beautiful parallels between the giving of God's Commandments and the giving of God's Spirit. On both occasions, Shavuot becomes the day when heaven is opened and God Himself claims His people.

The Great Day of Pentecost.

After Jesus' death, when the disciples were hiding fearing arrest after Jesus' execution they gathered to celebrate the Feast of Pentecost, together with Jesus' mother, Mary. Scriptures says that Jesus told the Apostles:

*"**Remain here in the city until you are clothed with power from on high**". (Luke 24–49). Then:*

*"When the day of Pentecost came it found them gathered in one place. Suddenly from up in the sky there came a noise like a strong, driving wind which was heard through the house where they were gathered. Tongues of fire appeared which parted and came to rest on each of them. **All were filled with the Holy Spirit. They began to express themselves in foreign tongues and make bold proclamation as the Spirit prompted them**. (Acts 2:1–4)*

What an explosive and mind-blowing event! *"**Until you are clothed with power from on high.**"*

It sounds unreal, dramatic; it must have caused pandemonium among those present. We can imagine the frightening scene as the strong wind blew in their midst, blowing curtains, ruffling hair, and extinguishing whatever candles were lit. And then adding to this phenomenal scene, there appeared threatening flames which made them realize this was all an act of God fulfilling Jesus' promise to send them the Holy Spirit.

It was, in effect, a supernatural occurrence. Like the burning bush that met Moses. The effects of this event were considered the earth-shaking event for the followers of Christ.

The down pouring of the Holy Spirit was an explosive event complete with fireworks and flashes which directly empowered the disciples with extraordinary boldness and spiritual gifts that changed the course of the world. Christianity was born!

In a real way, the gift of the Holy Spirit promised by Jesus came true, spiritual Power upon the disciples. This was the Power of Pentecost, individually transmitted to each Apostle. This feast brought Jews to Jerusalem from all over the land and it was not difficult to gather a crowd. The Apostles spoke in tongues that were understood by everyone, irrespective of the region they came from.

The Bible account is incredibly powerful.

Later, after leaving the room where they had met for the Pentecostal feast and where they experienced the down pouring of the Holy Spirit, Simon Peter made a powerful discourse to the Jewish crowd:

> *"It was to you and your children that the promise was made and to all those still far off whom the Lord our God calls... Save yourselves from this generation which has gone astray." Those who accepted his message were baptised; some three thousand were added that day. (Acts 2:39–41)*

St Paul found that the Church in Corinth was divided over spiritual gifts given to it by God. Paul reminds the Church that all the gifts are given by the same God and should be used to help the Church, rather than to divide it.

Paul says the gifts include wisdom, knowledge, healing, miraculous powers, and prophecy. Such gifts should be used positively and for the common good (1 Cor. 12:1–15). All these gifts emanated from that first Christian Pentecost.

Through the Power of Pentecost this is indeed the gifts which come to those who accept Jesus into their hearts and now live in the Spirit of the Lord like a tree planted near running water.

Psalm 1.

"Happy the man who follows not the counsel of the wicked nor walks in the way of sinners, nor sits in the company of the insolent, but delights in the law of the Lord and meditates on his law day and night. He is like a tree planted near running water that yields it fruit in due season and whose leaves never fade, whatsoever he does, prospers." (Psalm 1).

Again, here lies the power of Pentecost!

> *When Paul says, "My old self has been crucified with Christ. It is no longer I who lives, but Christ lives in me. So I live in this earthly body by trusting in the Son of God, who loved me and gave himself for me"* (Gal. 2:20).

They say that most of us are born with our eyes closed and go through life still with our eyes closed. Such was I. The Prince of this world took me to the mountaintop and showed me his riches; I took it all. I now realise that at the time I thought I had everything, yet in truth, I had nothing! A life without God is empty!

I am truly aware that there will be many who know me that will be very surprised at reading this personal testimony, but as I have said before, the Lord works wonders, he certainly worked wonders with me.

My hope is that this short book will remind and reinforce readers of the truth of several important relevant subjects and also help to evangelize by throwing some light as to what has made the Catholic Church great and enduring over the centuries, even when religious and frugal conflicts abounded and many institutions, monarchies, and empires perished. Yet the Apostolic Catholic Church, even with an earth-shaking Reformation, remained and continued to grow. The Church, though composed of sinners, "For we have all sinned and fall short of the Glory of God", is Holy.

The start of Joe's Religious Inclinations.

I have nil religious credentials, but to give readers an idea of my involvement in Church matters,

In the following chapters I recount some of my experiences of my humble spiritual pilgrimage.

To start with the following are from a letter written in 1984 by my Parish priest, Father John McNamee (RIP) to Bishop O'Byrne of the Diocese of Calgary.

Father John wrote to the Bishop informing him that I had been a member of his Parish for the last two years and was actively involved as an auxiliary Eucharistic Minister, a reader, facilitator for the Bible study group which Joe had initiated. He was Chairman of religious education and Communication, and a Mission awareness facilitator for MAC 6. Joe was also attending the TEAM (Together Enabling Adults in Ministry) course at the F.C.J. Centre since January 1984. And that I was known to Fathers Gerry, Gratian, and Bastigal.

Father John noted that I had been approached by the Franciscan Association for Catholic Evangelization to work with them to sponsor the *Glory of God* TV programme, which was planned to be shown on Spokane Television Channel 8. The purpose of the transmission was to reach virtually the whole of Alberta parts of eastern British Columbia and the Spokane, Washington, area, an audience of approximately 1.5 million households. This programme was first televised over Christmas 1984 and for two subsequent years. In preparation for the TV programme I visited the FACE (Franciscan Association for Catholic Evangelization) headquarters in Dallas, Texas.

He also noted that F.A.C.E wanted the Bishop's consent to the project. Father John mentioned that FACE would not air any of its programmes over any territory without the blessing of the local bishop.

He also shared that I was arranging to bring Father John Bertolluci, one of F.A.C.E.'s well-known Catholic preachers, to a rally I was organising in Calgary in the spring of 1985.

Father John mentioned that I would like to visit with Bishop O'Byrne for a few minutes to expand on this matter should he so require. This visit to Bishop O'Bryne was eventually not required, and he granted his approval of my projects.

Father John concluded his letter by saying I had standing in our Catholic community that it was a recommendation he was personally very pleased to give.

At the time I was undertaking a two-year spiritual and theological study at the FCJ Centre, in Calgary, as mentioned previously. This course prepared laypeople to serve as lay Ministers. It was under the tutelage of several Religious Sisters and Priests who taught spirituality, scripture study, apologetics, liturgical studies, and Church history.

In retrospect, I realize that my interest and involvement in spiritual matters increased in proportion with the change in my marriage and my dwindling finances. I was seeing thousands upon thousands of dollars, held in various investments go down the drain, money that had come from the sale of my business to a huge Belgium conglomerate, Societe General de Belgique. Incredibly I was cool and almost unaffected as these events took place. I placed my predicament in God's hands. But it felt as if the good Lord was sparing me from the ordeal and pain that a separation usually brings and was instead compensating me by filling my heart, mind, and life with spiritual things. I was fully conscious of this. In fact, in a strange way, I now reflect I was feeling fulfilled with my changes in life and the closeness to God.

The Life of Job?

My brother, Bishop Charles Caruana, told me that my life experiences reminded him of the trials of Job, a life of prosperity followed by hard times. My life was certainly a fast rollercoaster experience, but Job's was worse than mine and more exemplary. But in the end, both, through faith, ended in close friendship with God.

Principally He showed me the meaning to my life, rearranging my priorities and giving me direction. He was putting me through a purification process of renewal and of emptying in a way I never thought possible. Effortlessly turning me away from sinfulness and towards an ever growing search for God's Spiritual gifts.

But above all He has helped me to see Christ in others.

My Catholic Evangelical Path.

I started to get involved in a stream of evangelical endeavours within the Catholic Church. However I was not conscious of this at the time I was driven by winds I was not aware of. As I grew in the love of Jesus, I was saddened to seeing how frequently situations of de-Christianization happened in our lives, leading to the innumerable number of people baptized but who lived outside the Christian life, like my former self. I belonged to the "hatch, batch, and dispatch club", meaning that my church, attendances were confined to christenings, Weddings, and funerals." I chose to be a person with a certain faith but imperfect knowledge. I listened to intellectuals who felt the need to know Jesus Christ in a different light, thereby exposing faith to secularisation and, at times, militant atheism.

My faith was exposed to many trials and threats. It was a Faith besieged and actively opposed, not by strangers but by my proper self.

I realized I was surrounded by a horrendous increase in unbelief in the modern world with the drama of "atheistic humanism" and "hedonism" which preaches there is no need for God that God is superfluous, and that God has even become an encumbrance. A belief that recognizes the power of humankind by denying God and that pleasure must be clasped at every opportunity. Luckily, I was aware of all these happenings and I was certainly not going to succumb.

But there is another virus going around which is spiritually killing hundreds of millions of people. That is secularism and atheism. This virus also requires a spiritual vaccine to return the world to a spiritually healthy place. That vaccine is called the Good News of Christ! The seed of the love of Jesus needs to re-germinate throughout the earth, like the flames of Pentecost, to set it on fire, with kindness and the love of Christ.

I want to fight against the former trend by standing up for my faith because my faith runs the risk of perishing from suffocation or starvation if it is not fed and sustained each day. In this book I am, in a way, attempting to evangelize, to provide some background knowledge of a brave and fighting church, not as a group of men but as gladiators of the Faith. So brave that during the first and third centuries, when Christianity was in its infancy and persecuted over 2.53 million Christians, or 31.5 per cent of the then-known world, died for their faith! Today over 70 million Christians have been martyred. Such losses have not held back the growth of Christianity. In fact, Christianity, though in flux, is growing universally, and Jesus' promise is being fulfilled, "I will ask the Father, and He will give you another Advocate to be with you forever" (John 14:17).

All Are Called to Evangelize

The call to evangelize started when Jesus, on one occasion, when He had been with the Apostles, he said to them:

"You will receive power when the Holy Spirit comes down on you, then you are to be my witnesses in Jerusalem throughout Judea and Samaria, yes even to the ends of the earth". (Acts 1: 8)

So what encourages me to do this? I have read Pope Paul VI's 1975 message in *Evangelli Nunciani (Announcing the Good News)*. He wrote:

> "Those who have received the Good News and who have been gathered into the community of salvation can and must Communicate and Spread it" (E.N. 13).

This apostolic exhortation continues:

> "Who then has the mission of Evangelizing? It falls upon all the Church by divine command to go to the whole world to proclaim the Good News to the entire World. The whole Church is Missionary it is the basic duty of the People of God" (E.N. 59).

We may ask what then can you and I do for our faith? My reply comes from the Holy Father's same document:

> "We would not wish to end this encounter with our beloved brethren and sons and daughters without a pressing appeal concerning the interior attitudes which must emanate those who work for evangelization.
>
> In the name of the Lord Jesus Christ, and in the name of the Apostles Peter and Paul, we wish to exhort all those who, thanks to the Charismas of the Holy Spirit and to the mandate of the Church, are true Evangelizers worthy of this vocation, to exercise it without the reticence of doubt or fear, and not to neglect the conditions that will make this evangelization not only possible but also active and fruitful. These, among many others, are the fundamental conditions which we consider important to emphasize. (E.N.74)
>
> This is our desire too, and we exhort all evangelizers, whoever they may be, to pray without ceasing to the Holy Spirit with faith and fervour and to let them prudently be guided by Him as the decisive inspirer of their plans, their initiatives and their evangelizing activity. (E.N.75).

"Who ever they may be." I took it to mean me. I realized that when Jesus sent His Apostles to be witnesses to the World, this included me and you, ordinary laypersons, in order to proclaim the good the Lord has done in our lives. It has been my experience that the testimonies of ordinary individuals are some of the most effective ways of evangelizing. It is true that *"Faith comes from hearing and hearing the Word of God" (Romans 10:17)*, but to hear individual personal witnesses to what Christ has done in their lives is doubly effective to listeners.

Kerygma is the Word. It means "to proclaim the Good News of Jesus Christ". As I read these words and other apostolic exhortations as I was going through several traumatic events, such as a severe heart attack and a marriage break-down an attempted business blackmail by a disgruntled ex-employee and former friend. Plus, importantly took there was an economic downturn in Canada's gas and oil industry owing to oil prices crashing. Many businesses around me were going under. I could have easily turned to alcohol or drugs or searched for solace in the female gender. But no, I decided to turn to God in an ever-increasing manner and put my shoulder to the work of my Church.

I now look back with satisfaction at my contributions to evangelization. I would like you to join me in recalling some of these experiences. It has become a spiritual journey full of satisfaction.

2
CHAPTER

Some Personal Experiences

The purpose of this chapter is to give the reader a brief idea of my humble spiritual journey, which I recorded at the time these events occurred.

It started sometime in 1983, the year my brother had open heart surgery in London, and I had a 'change of heart. I told my brother, *"You know Charles you must be the richest man on earth. I wish I had just a teeny-weeny bit of the love these people have for you."*

His reply was simply, "And why not?"

The events I am recounting gladly filled my life with meaning.

My initial purpose was to write about the Power in our Hands and a short account of my experience with the Eucharist, but now in my eighty-fourth birthday—or as some say in the sunset of my life, I desire to leave a record of these experiences. To borrow a phrase used in the Christian Cursillo Movement, I decided to write this book as if, "bailing out of the plane without a parachute", and, shooting from the hip, with both guns blaring. And with no shame for allowing God to come into my heart and talking about him.

Late in life I realized that life is what happens to you while you're busy making other plans. In the course of our everyday lives, something happens that vividly and unexpectedly summons us to union with God.

If we are in communion with God, we realize in a flash what it's all about. We weren't looking for it, but it found us. As we walk through life, be open to the inrushing tide of God's call, it happened that I gave everything up that was holding me back.

I look around my home and see the photos of all those beloved members of my family who have departed in the hope of a glorious resurrection they strongly believed this so since my life is coming to its inevitable end, I wish to give thanks and testify to a merciful and loving God. I give thanks for everything He has given me through His great love and grace, but particularly for the day He entered my life and for the gift of my family.

For my favourite short prayer, I borrowed from Mother Mary's Magnificat: "My soul magnifies the Lord and my spirit rejoices in God my Saviour for He has done great things for me, and holy is His name."

In the Storm Let Jesus Sleep

August 1983, and at 46 years of age, became a significant year in my life.

I simply cannot remember getting from London Heathrow Airport to St Mary's Hospital in Paddington; the journey was a blur. I arrived to find my brother hooked up to an intravenous drip and all kinds of seemingly ominous electric gadgets.

My sister and I sat next to his bed, praying together. I was holding my brother's hand, and half conscious still under the effects of the anaesthesia, he mumbled, "Joe, on the way to the operating theatre I offered this moment of pain and uncertainty to the Lord, for you, your wife and your marriage. That God may bless your family."

He was demonstrating his unselfish nature to us that day; he was thinking of us at a time when his own life was on the line. At that moment I knew I had to look seriously at my life and search for this peace and love that my brother so freely gives and receives.

Meanwhile, on that day all the churches in Gibraltar held a vigil during the hours of his operation. Jews, Protestants, and Muslims prayed for Charles's recovery that day. Heaven must have been bombarded with loving prayers for his well-being. He had to survive. God needed this special shepherd for his flock, and his work was not yet completed. God responded positively.

Little did I know that this prayer of mine would one day be answered.

He had just come out of surgery and he said that before the operation this vivid story came to mind, in 1983 open heart surgery was yet in its infancy and for several reasons many surgeries had ended in mortal failure,

Before his traumatic episode, Charles told us how worried and frightened he had been. He said that he recalled the occasion when Jesus and His Disciples were crossing the Sea of Galilee

When a terrible storm blew up and His Disciples, all of them seasoned fishermen and accustomed to bad weather, were quite shaken so severe was the storm that they looked to Jesus, who was asleep in the bow of the boat. In their panic they woke up Jesus. They were sure they would all drown. Jesus woke and rebuked them, saying, "Where is your courage? How little faith you have".

Charles told us that the open heart operation surgery had taken on a different meaning for him.

He had resolved that no matter how frightened he might be, no matter how dangerous this surgery was, he was not going to cry out for help to Jesus. Instead, he said he would, "Let Jesus sleep."

I wondered *how you can let Jesus sleep at a moment like this*. I realized that I was trying to find myself through my own stormy passage where I thought that Jesus must have surely been asleep.

The procedure of doing seven bypasses was unheard off. It was even considered debilitating, yet Charles recovered very well after several months of convalescence. He continued his fifty-four years of priestly life with eighteen years of these as the energetic Bishop of Gibraltar.

The Hotel Room

The time came for me to make the decision of leaving the family home and starting the process of my marital separation, a very stormy passage in my life, I went to a nearby hotel. I was broken and completely depressed.

Never in a thousand years did I ever think that my marriage would break up. So the situation was that I, in 1983, was emotionally broken and so damaged that it was difficult to think how I could recover.

The choices before me, as I saw them, were harsh, revenge, curse and blaspheme, which of these employed the heaviest retribution? Or was suicide the easiest way-out?

None of these since I was heavily to blame for the weakening of my marriage.

I sat on the edge of the hotel bed with a bottle of whisky close at hand, minus three inches of the heady liquid. I looked to the side and caught a glimpse of a Gideon Bible sitting on the bedside table, kindly placed there by that great Missionary body. My sole purpose was to hide it. I reached out for the Good Book to put it in the drawer of the bedside table, out of sight its presence convicting me.

When I grasped the book, I noticed a bookmark poking out from the top of the book. Instinctively, instead of putting the book away, I opened it at the bookmark. I glanced at the page and took another drink from my glass. With my vision blurry from crying, I read the following incredible passage:

> *Save me, O God, for the waters threaten m life; I am sunk in the abysmal swamp where there is no foothold; I have reached the watery depths the flood overwhelms me. I am wearied with calling my throat is arched. My eyes have failed with looking for my God. Those outnumber the hair on my head that hate me without cause. O God, you know my folly, and my faults are not hid from you. (Psalm 69)*

Without realising it, I was reading Psalm 69, "A cry of anguish in great distress". — How strange the passage reflected my own heartfelt situation at the time. It seemed my world had fallen apart. I felt I was losing everything and everyone I loved. I had never experienced so much desolation, rejection and dejection. In this period of rejection, which fell on the twenty-fifth anniversary of our marriage, I felt that no one loved or cared for me.

I continued reading the Bible, and every line jumped out at me. The Bible came alive in my hands. Jesus' parable of the fig tree came alive. From a distance, the fig tree was lush, green, and full of leaves. It looked so promising, but it had no figs, no fruit! I drew analogies between the fig tree and my life; that was me, I thought, all lush leaves and no fruit, only appearances.

A ray of light started to shine within me. I realized that I had led a life without God and without spiritual fruits. I had experienced and taken another step in my personal journey of change. I realized I had another and better option, to seek God.

I went to confession, started to attend Mass, and began to receive Holy Communion. That small Gideon Bible had started me off on a great journey. I wondered if this was one of the ways God operates— unnoticed, under the radar, on the edge of my life, not drawing attention to Him.

I came to understand that God's delay in answering was not God's denial to my prayers, mine and your prayer will be answered in God's own time, faith is spelled, "P-a-t-i-e-n-c-e" which means hope more and thereby suffer less.

God Plays Snooker

I always smile when I think how God, always responds, to those who are faithful to him, despite the many times we try to control and manipulate our affairs and commit so many and mistakes and blunders, He always turns every event around even when they appear to be disastrous, God always turns them into something beneficial for us.

At the time I was totally immersed in my business and hurting from my marital situation. One day I received in the mail a card from the post office instructing me to come and pick up a parcel. As I drove to my office, I placed the card on the passenger seat of my car. As I drove around, it appeared that the card fell to the side off the seat and out of sight.

A month or so later, as I opened the passenger door, the card fell out. I picked it up and very surprised, I hastily drove to the post office to collect the parcel. I had no idea who or from where it had come.

I handed the card to the gentleman behind the counter. Ten minutes later he came out and informed me that the parcel had been returned to sender. Still puzzled, I asked him if he could possibly tell me from where and who sent the parcel.

Several minutes transpired, the man came back with a small notebook and read out to me that the parcel was actually a 'cylinder container' and that it had come from Vatican City, Rome. The sender was His Holiness the Pontiff!

What? What could His Holiness, the Pope, have sent me? I had no idea.

That evening, with an 8 hour time difference, I telephoned my brother, Charles across the Atlantic, and put this riddle to him. Why would the Pope send me something in a postal cylinder?

"Oh", he exclaimed. "That must have been the papal blessing certificate for your twenty-fifth wedding anniversary. I applied for it for you some time ago."

A papal blessing that I never received! Of course how could it since my marriage, in reality, had broken down a few months earlier, there was really no longer a wedding anniversary to celebrate, so, no papal blessing.

Coincidence or God incidence? You decide.

Another of God's Snooker Games

I am convinced that it was the Power of Pentecost, or the Holy Spirit that led my two daughters, Suzanne and Lorraine, to invite me to attend a service to hear an American evangelical preacher at a Pentecostal church in North Calgary to which they attended. I was told this preacher was a young and dynamic speaker well known in evangelical circles.

I reluctantly accompanied my daughters to this event. We sat close to the raised podium. Music came from an enthusiastic group, and everyone sung and praised the Lord. It was a most enjoyable moment. The guest preacher, Bob Road (not his real name), from the United States, was introduced.

As he walked onto the podium, the preacher made a big impression on the congregation. He was young, good-looking, very well dressed from top to bottom, and smiled a lot. His shoes were bright and highly polished. His hair and matching collar and tie were perfectly in place.

He gave an excellent oratory, complete with spiritual rhetoric. I knew a wasted politician when I saw one because I had been one.

Everything was going well, with the congregation fully captivated by his passionate presentation. At one point he dealt on the subject of the devil, and somehow he connected this with the Catholic Church and the Virgin Mary. He went into the tirade about the Pope's connection with the Mafia, and so on.

As he spoke, I sank deeper in my seat. What I was hearing was blasphemy to my ears. What ignorance, what fabrication, what distortions coming from a Christian preaching Christian love. I had never heard so much ignorant rubbish.

When the preacher finished his talk, he received a standing ovation. Many came down to the podium to congratulate him and proudly patted him on the back. I could not do less than these people.

I too got up and went forward to where the preacher was, surrounded by all these enthusiastic people. I stood there in front of him, but I did not pat him on the back. Instead, I pointed at his face and said to him, "Brother, you are void of the Holy Spirit. No Christian who lives by the Holy Spirit would talk about another Christian Church like you have just done. No Christian talks about Mary, the mother of God, in that way. You have closed a door, and it is obvious you do not know what you are talking about!"

Frankly, I expected to be bodily taken out of the place. I was soon separated from the preacher and gently directed to the door. There was a rumpus, and several people called me names that I did not catch, "Go to the devil", was one thing I heard.

I left the packed auditorium, got into my Mercedes 450 SLC, and sped home, about ten miles away. I was naturally shaken and unsettled. I feared that I would, as punishment, crash my car and pay the penalty for my bravado.

It was past midnight when I got home. I made myself a cup of tea and sat down to compose myself and gather my thoughts. I had no one at hand to share what happened, so I picked up the phone and called my brother in Gibraltar on the other side of the Atlantic. It must have been 8 a.m. in Gibraltar, pretty early, but Charles was an early riser. He picked up the phone on the second ring. "What're you up to, Joe, calling at this late hour of the day?" It was late hour for me, but early for him.

I recounted what happened and asked him if I had done right or wrong. His answer was short and clear. "Joe, in the first place, you were very brave to stand up in public and defend your faith. In the second place, you did the right thing. I advise you to go to your parish church. When I was there last, I saw a notice inviting people to a Charismatic prayer meeting. I am sure that if you share your experience with them, they will be able to help you in some way or another."

Frankly, I had not visited my local church at all and had never heard of the charismatic movement.

I found this advice a strange way of helping me referring me to a group of people I did not know. I placed no hope in this advice of his.

The following day, a Monday, I stopped outside the church and read the notice board: "Charismatic Movement meets every Tuesday at 7 p.m. All are welcomed."

I took note.

My First Charismatic Exposure.

That Thursday I attended the meeting I confess I had never attended a prayer meeting such as this, held in the basement of the church proper, it felt a little strange. But as soon as I walked in I smelled the coffee!

I was made most welcome and shook hands all-round. I felt better since everyone there was smiling. I might even say they glowed with friendship as they, talked and moved about in an ambience of joviality. At least the hospitality was impeccable.

We all sat in the pre-arranged circle of chairs. There were approximately thirty persons present, so this involved a lot of warm hand-shaking.

After welcoming the new-comer, me, to the group, someone invoked the presence of the Holy Spirit, "Come Holy Spirit and fill the heart of thy faithful and enkindle in them the fire of Your Love and send forth Your Spirit and we will be recreated ..."

Wow, what a take-off.

Then someone read a section from the Holy Bible: "Can you not realize that the unholy will not fall heir to the kingdom of God? Do not deceive yourselves, any fornicators, idolaters, or adulterers, no sodomites, thief's misers, or drunkards, no slanderers or robbers will inherit Gods kingdom." And such were some of you; but you have been washed, consecrated, justified in the name of our Lord Jesus Christ and in the Spirit of our God." (1Cor: 6, 9-11.). And without the help of the Holy Spirit no one can say, "Jesus is Lord."

"There are different kinds of gifts. But they are all given to believers by the same Spirit. There are different ways to serve. But they all come from the same Lord. There are different ways the Spirit works. But the same God is working in all these ways and in all people.

The Holy Spirit is given to each of us in a special way. That is for the good of all. To some people the Spirit gives a message of wisdom. To others the same Spirit gives a message of knowledge. To others the same Spirit gives faith. To others that one Spirit gives gifts of healing. To others he gives the power to do miracles. To others he gives the ability to prophesy. To others he gives the ability to tell the spirits apart. To others he gives the ability to speak in different kinds of languages they had not known before. And to still others he gives the ability to explain what was said in those languages. All the gifts are produced by one and the same Spirit. He gives gifts to each person, just as he decides." (1 Cor.12:4-11).

It seemed everyone present, except me, had an open Bible with them, I thought that was very good but it was very rare in a Catholic group. Then they shared their thoughts about what had been read from the scriptures.

The realization that I could be the recipient of these marvellous spiritual gifts was new to me, but I wanted them badly.

And then someone read the parable of the prodigal son! This whole moment was an incredible personal experience for me; every word was etched in my mind.

When that reading was over a few persons started playing guitars and everyone sung joyful praise songs to their hearts content.

I tried to follow the songs on the huge T.V. screen attached to a wall. As I looked around I saw everyone had their arms raised. The smiling continued unabated, I too sang with my hands and arms almost outstretched, in the 'Oran' position, eyes closed.

I had never prayed like that before but praying with outstretched arms came to me as second nature.

When the singing finished they turned the meeting over to individual prayers of thanksgiving and praise.

Some prayed out loud in a language I did not understand, some of the present were Ukrainians, Germans, Polish or whatever. Maybe they were praying in their native tongue. The fact was that I could not follow what they were saying.

Then they asked if there was anyone who needed prayers; I stood up and waved my arm to indicate I needed prayers. A few came to me and asked me to sit down. After I did, they placed their hands over my head, covering it but not touching me. I closed my eyes and prayed internally. The strange language continued to be spoken, by all those standing over me.

I felt secure and, above all, protected. With a warm feeling within me I started to weep unashamedly. Again I heard strange voices softly praying,

As I continued to weep, someone said, *"Joe, God loves you, He is healing you, so surrender your concerns and fears to His love. Turn your problems over to Him. God loves you."*

"I will, I will." I replied, sobbing.

I felt God's presence and at home among these people.

Wow, what a take-off.

I knew for certain my brother had been right. He knew that my greatest need was to know God again.

My inner peace returned, and I resumed living without fear, I took to these meetings like a duck takes to water.

I was later informed that the praying in that strange language was actually "praying in tongues", well that was news to me, this was a gift of the Holy Spirit, and this too was news from Paul's letter to the Corinthians that someone had read earlier.

I continued to attend these Prayer Meetings at St. Bonaventure regularly and became an active member of the group.

I knew for certain my brother had been right, he knew that my greatest need was to know God again.

My inner peace returned and I resumed living without fears, I took to these meetings like a duck takes to water.

Had I become, at that point, a born-again-Catholic? Perhaps I had, I had been far removed from my Church and now I looked forward to these meetings and avidly read my bible. I was told that one of the first gifts of the Holy Spirit was a thirst for scripture, that was news to me as well, but I found out that it was true

The Diocese Breakfast Meetings.

I integrated well with this group. But now I was not only going to Sunday Mass and weekly Prayer meetings but several weeks later, I was invited to a Diocesan Breakfast Prayer meeting, that meant that the 24 Charismatic prayer groups of the 24 parishes of the Diocese of Calgary met every month on a Saturday morning for prayers and exhortation, this was held at the Marriot Hotel in Calgary, Canada, morning

I had been invited to form part of the 'Intercession' team who would stand up in front of the podium and lay hands and pray for those who came forward for prayer.

When the breakfast was over a teaching, from a passage of the bible, was delivered by one of the senior person there. After the 'Teaching' there followed some 'Praise' singing and then people started to come forward to an 'Altar-Call' for people came forward and stood in a line in front of me, I place my hands over their heads and prayed, I evidenced that people, in front of me, with a prayerful and peaceful smile on their faces, they went into a state of, what is called, *"resting in the spirit"*, a peaceful, tranquil state, some swayed with a gentle tremor, knees slackened and some fell gently to the floor helped by other persons standing close by, who caught them as they fell and safely allowed them to lay peacefully on the floor.

As the praying went on I felt an unusual warmth spreading through the palms of my hands, and when people approached for the imposition of hands the warmth slowly increased from warm to very warm, almost hot.

I was amazed and filled with a mixture of wonder and disbelief at this happening, it was happening to me, to the point where I questioned how God could allow this to happen through my unworthy intervention. It made me feel very humble and inadequate but it also made me think about the power that flows through the hands of normal men and women allowing them to do the work for God, which helped these persons to grow in their faith.

I was invited to many Prayer meetings held in the different parishes of the Diocese and the surrounding towns and cities.

At a different Breakfast Prayer Meeting held in Calgary I was invited to take part in the intercessory team and therefore I took my place in the front line with about six other persons.

The music played and the guest speaker invited people to come forward, in an Altar-call to receive special personal prayers.

People started to come forward and a line formed in front of me. As I prayed over the many persons who came for praying-over I got the a warm sensation in my hands, it was such a powerful sensation that I was actually overcome with this wondrous feeling, I would like to think it was a sensation of 'anointing', the heat got so strong that I felt I had to leave the premises and go out to the garden to seat and compose myself since I felt so humble.

The Businessmen Prayer Meetings.

I found out that there was such a thing as a Businessmen's Prayer meeting where members of various denominations got together to pray, as a Catholic I could not fail to attend. It too met once a month luckily this was during a weekday morning. This were also very successful, hundreds of businessmen met before going to work, men of all professions and trades.

I soon found out that Businessmen Breakfast Prayer Meetings were held in almost every great City in Canada and the USA, this too was an exciting revelation.

The story goes that way back in 1857 a business man by the name of Jeremiah Lapkin felt that there was a need to create an environment where business men could meet for prayers. This happened in a location in Fulton Street.

This inspired other business men to meet all around USA and Canada.

I was so excited when I heard about these meetings that I soon started to go to them on a monthly basis.

There was one to which I felt compelled to go to this Businessman meeting took place in the USA.

Many famous men, in the USA and Canada, attended these meetings.

President Obama and Tony Blair attended it, while Blair was still Prime Minister of Britain.

When Obama's time came to speak he said, among many other things: *"Faith is the great cure for fear."*

Blair after 10 years as Prime Minister, besides other things said at that same Prayer meeting:

"There are many frustrations – that is evident. There is also one blessing. I spend much of my time in the Holy Land and in the Holy City. The other evening I climbed to the top of Notre Dame in Jerusalem. You look left and see the Garden of Gethsemane. You look right and see where the Last Supper was held. Straight ahead lays Golgotha. In the distance is where King David was crowned and still further where Abraham was laid to rest. And of course in the centre of Jerusalem is the Al Aqsa Mosque, where according to the Qur'an, the Prophet was transported to commune with the prophets of the past. Rich in conflict, it is also sublime in history. The other month in Jericho, I visited the Mount of Temptation. I think they bring all the political leaders there. My guide – a Palestinian – was bemoaning the travails of his nation. Suddenly he stopped, looked heaven wards and said "Moses, Jesus, Mohammed: why did they all have to come here?"

I was familiar with what the marvellous works the disciples of Jesus had gone through in the Acts of the Apostles but, this was the 21st Century, certainly not the days of the Apostles.

Yet throughout the ages, as shown in the writings of both the Old and the New Testaments Bibles, God's love for human-kind, uses the hands and the mouths of sinful men and women to carry out his work of salvation on this earth. Simply because with His Incarnation He brought Heaven to this earth of ours.

As is evidenced in the Hebrew Bible ordinary men and women, such as Abraham, Moses, Isaiah, Zachariah and others become God's currency or instruments initiating people to meet God in everyday ordinary life, as the song says, *'make me a channel of your love'*. He makes people currencies and vehicles for His 'Good News'; in this way people can find God through you and me.

Through the Sacraments, which are the visible signs of the Spiritual reality, God uses men as Heralds, to proclaim God's message and we, who receive this message, become His Messengers, at the service to the World in a mission of salvation.

The Church does not depend solely on my efforts but on the unwarranted power that God, through His Holy Spirit, desires to give to His Messengers, that is you and me.

My life story, and yours, and where we are today, is a beautiful piece of God's work, working in us, in spite of our shortcomings, our mistakes and our sinfulness.

Therefore in gratitude for everything that the LORD has done in my life I borrow some of Mother Mary's words from the Magnificat, *"My soul magnifies the LORD and my spirit rejoices in GOD my Saviour for he has done great things for me and Holy is HIS name."* (Luke 1: 46-49. NAB).

Several years later, when I had returned to my home town of Gibraltar and joined the Charismatic Renewal Groups a close friend of mine Charles Harrison initiated the Gibraltar branch of the Businessmen Prayer Meetings to which I joyfully attended, but by then I was fully involved with my own mission at Camp Emmanuel helping Drug Addicts and Alcoholics. However for reasons I do not know these Breakfast meetings ceased to be held.

I Revisit the Pentecostal Church in Calgary.

In the meantime back in my office, my secretary gave me several messages that a gentleman, a Mr Lagore, had sent saying that he would like to speak with me. The name was not familiar to me, so I ignored these messages.

At a meeting I had with my daughter Lorraine the name of her Pastor came up, Pastor Lagore!

I called Pastor Lagore and excused myself for the delay in getting back to him. How could I help him?

He invited me to lunch. During lunch he apologized for what had happened several weeks ago with Preacher Bob Road. He told me the elders of the church at a meeting in their church, agreed that preacher Road's references to the Catholic Church on the evening of my visit were inappropriate, and their Church elders wanted to apologize to me for that incident, several weeks past, and let me know they had the utmost respect for the Catholic Church.

Since I spoke fluent Spanish he invited me to meet with his Church's group of Hispanics, who happened to have a weekly TV programme called *Amor Latino*, broadcasted on Sundays. I was introduced as, "Joe, a Charismatic Catholic businessman friend and guest."

This was God's marvellous "white ball" falling into the net. It had turned an unpleasant situation into a joyous event. Over the years we maintained a harmonious relationship, a Catholic Charismatic with a Pentecostal Church. Talk about playing snooker!

Meeting Two Saints, In Rome.

Joe grasping Pope John Paul II's hand

I visited Rome in 1984 as a delegate to the Sixth International Leaders Conference of: The Catholic Charismatic Renewal Movement, Indeed a visit in the style of the Power of Pentecost.

This conference coincided with the twentieth anniversary of the creation of the Catholic Charismatic Renewal Movement in 1964.

It turned out to be a grandiose, spiritually rich week that changed and filled my life with good things. I had come from Canada for this event.

I met so many spiritually rich and excellent speakers: Bishop Paul Cordes; Padre Fio Mascarenhas, SJ; Pedro Caetano de Tillesse, PP Brazil; Fr. Oscar Abauarantine, Sri Lanka; P. Rene Laurentin, France;

Cardinal Leon Suenens, Belgium; P. Diego Jaramillo, Colombia; Jean Vanier, L'Ache France/Canada; Ms. Marie Delaporte, France; Sr Linda Koonz, USA; Cardinal E. Pironio, the Vatican; Pius Okong, Uganda; and of course Pope John Paul II, and Mother Teresa of Calcutta. Both of these were eventually earned a well deserved Sainthood.

Almost seven hundred delegates from the whole world attended. The theme of the Conference was "Good News to the Poor" (Luke 4:18).

The conference and its participants were in high spirits. There was a great feeling of enthusiasm and expectation. I have never felt so much enthusiasm.

There I joined the Gibraltar contingent of about eight persons, including Susan Cruz, Mari Carmen, Adela Abrines, Louis Lombard, Albert Trinidad, Albert Brooks and his wife and Fr Paul Bear and others.

St John Paul II and St Mother Teresa

Mother Teresa of Calcutta spoke to our group. This very tiny person, feeble-looking nun, with very wrinkled skin, her hands perpetually clasped in prayer, exuded such a holy anointing that it was impossible not to feel. Her presence brought tears and joy to our eyes. She asked us to pray and do good in the world, so when we came into the presence of the Father, He would ask us not, "how much we'd done but rather, about how much love we had put into our actions".

"Hunger today is not for bread but for love." She added, "A work of love is a work of peace. The fruit of faith is love. The fruit of love is service and the fruit of service is peace. A clean heart will see God, and if we see God in other we will see God everywhere."

She told us the story of a dying man she had picked up in the street. Maggots were eating his flesh. She took him to Kalighat, an abandoned Hindu temple that she had made the headquarters of the Order Missionaries of Charity. They cleaned him of the maggots, but he died while she held his hand. Mother Teresa said that was probably the one time in his life when he had experienced human warmth.

Michelangelo's marble statue, The Pietà (*Mary holding the body of the dead Christ; Courtesy of* Wikipedia)

That same day, Louis Lombard, Albert Trinidad, and I walked into the great Basilica of St Peters.

To the right was the Michelangelo's marvellous sculpture *The Pietà*, which depicts Jesus' mother, Mary, holding in her lap the crucified Christ, recently lowered from the cross. We starred at it in awe. It seemed so real, that as we gazed at it, the body of Christ seemed to be sliding down, from its mother's knees, to the ground, giving each of us the desire to reach out and prevent the body from falling. It was a mystical sensation.

From there we moved a few yards along and we came to the "Chapel of Perpetual Adoration", where two nuns knelt in front of the Blessed Sacrament in prayer. The process of praying was continuous, day and night.

The three of us were touched at seeing and feeling the aura of holiness. We knelt and prayed with the two devoted sisters.

The following day we had an audience with Pope John Paul II. Mother Teresa joined him during our audience which was a meeting of loud prayers, praising, and singing. The Holy Father said to us, "The Charismatic *Renewal* is the eloquent manifestation of the youthful vitality of the Holy Spirit. A bold statement of what the Spirit is telling the Church."

Then, Cardinal Suenens addressed us and said, "Actually the Renewal is not a Movement; it is a Move of the Holy Spirit."

Later we moved to the great audience hall where the Holy Father, John Paul II sang with us and swayed with the music, his arms outstretched. The song "Vive Jesus el Senor" was sung, for the first time, in that Vatican Hall, with the Holy Father singing along with the two thousand or more delegates.

As he walked around the huge meeting hall, he came over to me. As he stretched his arms towards me, I managed to hold his hands in mine.

He had told us, "The Holy Spirit is your strength and your special treasure. I ask you, and all the members of the Charismatic Renewal, to continue to cry out aloud to the world with me, 'Open the doors to the Redeemer.' Be deeply united to the Mother Church. The Spirit prompts us in good faith to go forth to the poor and the poor-in-Spirit who are the little ones in the world."

In another hall we were met by Mother Teresa, I was about two metres from her, from her closeness I could feel her warm anointing radiating to me. She addressed us saying, "Hunger today is not for bread but for love. Work of love is a Work of Peace, a clean heart will see God, and if we see God in others we will see God Himself. Holiness is not the luxury of the few but the simple duty of each one of us." Beautiful words from a saint!

Two Angels

A healing service was taking place at 9.30 the following morning. It was being led by the gifted Sister Linda Koontz, who came from the United States.

When I arrived, the Basilica was packed to capacity, so I found a nice quiet place at the back of the church; near me were two snow-white marble columns. At one point of the Healing service, Sister Linda asked everyone to extend our arms to the person closest to us.

To my right I noticed a black-skinned, slim, young man dressed in a white Dominican tunic. To my left was a young nun, petite and frail-looking, in a black robe. Both stood there praying. Almost simultaneously, they both looked at me, standing on my own, and caught my eye. They beckoned me with a smile. We closed ranks, and they laid their hands on my shoulders. One to my right the other to my left. They looked like a pair of porcelain Lladro figurines; two fragile figures holding up a heavy soul full of sorrow.

I felt special and privileged in my aloneness. I prayed God would pass on to me a little of the devotion and anointing of these two angels. The heaviness of my family situation was weighing me down. But now my heavy burden was being lifted by the nearness of these two. Yet I knew not their names, who they were, or where they came from. We did not say a single word to each other. They smiled at me, and I felt the warm anointing of their hands on my shoulders. Surely God had placed these two angels there for a reason. Was there a message and a purpose in this? I think there was. I was being told, "Joe, you are *not* alone!"

A few months later I would undergo a severe cardiac intervention, and a few months later I would cut my ties with Canada. I believe God was putting me to the test for my next enterprise, which was to set up a Christian drug Rehabilitation Centre for Gibraltar.

The New Pentecost: Cardinal Leo Joseph Suenens

However still in Rome, another highlight in this visit to Rome was meeting Cardinal Leo Joseph Suenens, who was the Archbishop of Mechelen-Brussels. He had been one of the four moderators of Vatican

Council II. He was also a fervent supporter of the Charismatic Movement that sprung up from Vatican II Council.

In 1974 he wrote his wonderful books *The New Pentecost* and *Renewal of the Powers of Darkness*. In 1986 he wrote *Controversial Phenomenon; Resting in the Spirit*.

Cardinal Suenens had undertaken an in-depth study of the phenomenon of resting in the Spirit, gathering opinions from many sources directly involved in the Charismatic Renewal.

The conclusion was that this matter had to be taken with a lot of discernment and caution since people could be easily influenced. Or as happens in evangelical circles, the resting was actually induced by touching the individual's forehead and giving a slight push when the person's eyes were closed, thereby producing a fake resting.

Since the visit to Rome was specifically on the occasion of the International Charismatic Renewal Conference, he was naturally a very welcomed guest speaker. Since 1984 I have kept all these quotations in my files Providentially, I am able publish them today (2021). Cardinal Suenens told us:

> Go into the heart of the Church and into the heart of the Prayer of the Church, where there is a priority for The Living Word. The words of the Apostles, into the Sacramental prayer in the Grace of Pentecost.

"Be a box of matches," he told us. In other words, we should set the world on fire for Christ.

Pope John Paul II declared jointly a Marian and a Pentecost year. Cardinal Suenens told us to "Stay deeply with the Old traditions of the Roman Catholic Church, be yourself in the Church. Be yourself with Mary and the Saints. Be deeply spiritual and be charismatically rooted there."

He sent a message to those Bishops, who were not present, saying,

> The Charismatic Renewal is the eloquent manifestation of the youthful vitality of the Spirit today. A bold statement of what the Spirit is telling the Church today.

The Renewal accepts the Powerful pressure of the Holy Spirit. Go into the heart of the Church. I would say to the Bishops Go into the Heart of the Renewal. The Renewal is not a Movement, what is it? It is a Move of the Spirit. A Spirit in the Spring-time of the Church.

The Cardinal's words stayed engraved in my heart. I determined I would do whatever I could to add a grain of sand to build Christ's Kingdom on Earth. Bishop Paul Cordes said,

"Rome spelled backwards means Amor, Love, and Christianity was the religion of Love, because God is all love ". Love in Latin is spelled 'Agape'.

Rome can release powerful forces. In the first centuries there were the early witnesses who hid in the Catacombs, who died in the gigantic Coliseum. So never tire, overcome all kinds of obstacles. Christ will be there to help you.

Faith and Light: Jean Vanier

The next meeting was held in the Vatican's Conference hall. All our meetings so far were given by many anointed and spiritual persons and had been highly enriching. But the one to come was by far the most exciting and moving story we had yet heard.

The next presentation was by Jean Vanier, philosopher, theologian, and son of a former French Canadian Governor General of Canada. This conference hall was naturally equipped with a multilingual translation system; I set my earphones to English.

As Jean Varnier told the story of how he had met someone whose father had died recently, and this man was left an orphan at the age of fifty-four, alone with no family or relatives. He man suffered from a mental disability. Here he was a grown adult, who had depended all his life on his elderly parents, now he had no one to care for him.

Jean, as he spoke, was devastated and broken. Everyone—and I mean all of the one thousand or more people in the audience—were in tears. Even Jean was crying as he spoke. I could not follow along because the English translator was also sobbing. So I decided to set my earphones on to the Spanish setting, but that translator too was sobbing to the point where the combination of my sobbing and the translator's sobbing, it became very difficult for me to follow. But the message came through.

Jean said that he decided to take this adult to his home. But the story did not end there. Jean and friends found that there were many persons in similar circumstances in Paris.

Jean was joined by Marie-Melee Mathieu, and in 1964 they founded 'Leached', the predecessor of Faith and Light which was founded in 1971.

This association founded 1,640 Faith and Light communities in fifty countries. They cater to people with intellectual disabilities, their families, and their friends, particularly young friends who meet together on a regular basis in a Christian spirit to share friendship, pray together, have parties, and celebrate life. This Spirit of service was an excellent idea since families who found themselves in this situation joined the association when their affected family members were still young, and they have grown up with this peer and family group. As a result, they are prepared in plenty of time for the day when their parents have grown old and are unable to care for them or until they depart this world.

In his later life, according to a press release from L'Arche USA, allegations were made against Jean, and an investigation, "reveals that Jean Vanier himself has been accused of manipulative sexual relationships and emotional abuse between 1970 and 2005, usually within a relational context where he exercised significant power and a psychological hold over the alleged victims." Even though he did not belong to a Religious Order it never-the-less tarnished his reputation as a theologian and everything that he had done before.

A few years later, from 1988 on, I had the privilege of working with and hosting many outings of the branch of Faith and Light, Gibraltar, at Emmanuel Camp.

> I venture to add that on the occasion of their first visits to the Camp, I, and a few other regular volunteer workers at the Camp were moved to tears just seeing the joy in the faces of both the children and their parents and how they enjoyed this very special occasion in the open, flowery fields visited by busy colourful butterflies, orchards laden with oranges and pear trees, from which they picked the fruits, the trees themselves hosted by a variety of bird life. Wherever possible, we attempted to organize a Eucharist service for our guests, and Mass was celebrated by the kindly Fr Paul Bear.

Padre Dario Bentancourt

Joe onstage with Padre Dario Bentancourt at the San Diego Conference

In 1985 I made a trip to San Diego, California, with the intention of attending a Charismatic Renewal conference at which several key speakers were scheduled to preach. One of them was Padre Dario Bentancourt, about whom I had learned about during my last visit to Gibraltar. I was told that a Father Dario Bentancourt had visited Gibraltar to preach at a Charismatic conference and that he was a gifted preacher and charismatic individual.

When I heard that he was preaching in San Diego, I resolved to go there and hear him preach. Little did I know what that would lead to?

It happened that I booked to stay in a frontline beach hotel but since I arrived early, I went around the grounds and another nearby hotel to explore the layout of this beautiful coastline.

I noticed a group of people sitting in a garden pool. Some were obviously priests, given that they were wearing the typical dog-collars, there were also a couple of nuns. I came to the conclusion that they must be participating in the Charismatic Conference.

I overheard them speaking in Spanish, so without much ado, I approached the group and said in Spanish, "Good morning, everyone. Am I right in assuming that you are here to attend the charismatic conference? I have come for this event."

They all looked up at me with wide smiles, probably my funny Gibraltarian accent. Gracefully they asked me to join them and invited me to have some refreshments. The priest, who invited me to join them, asked me where I came from, and I answered, "Canada".

"Really? No, no. Your Spanish accent is not from Canada," he replied.

"That's correct. I originally came from Gibraltar."

"Gibraltar?" inquired the priest. "I have been to Gibraltar and have many friends there."

"Then you must be Padre Dario Bentancourt?" I replied.

"That's correct, I am. How did you know my name?"

"My brother mentioned you to me."

"Your brother, and who might he be?" he asked.

"Father Caruana."

"Don't tell me you are really Padre Carlo Caruana's brother?"

"Indeed I am."

"Well how about that?" He then introduced me to the others around the table, and proceeded to tell them all about his visit to Gibraltar and the close friendship he had founded with my brother, the spiritual leader of the Gibraltar Charismatic Movement.

I was asked about my involvement in the Charismatic movement and they could not believe that I had travelled all the way from Calgary, Canada to San Diego in the extreme south of California.

After hearing about my involvement and my close association with the Franciscan Association for Catholic Evangelization, Father Dario told me, "Joe, I would like you to form part of our guest speakers at tonight's conference in the auditorium. This auditorium had a capacity for 15,000 visitors. So with great pleasure I addressed the audience in a fifteen-minute testimony of my life.

Father Dario was known as an itinerant preacher. He also had a popular radio programme, *Minuto de Dios*, broadcasted from Bogota, Columbia.

When Father Dario lived in New York City, he was the spiritual director of the Cursillo de Cristiandad. He later founded La Fundacion, Positivos Por la Vida, an outreach for underprivileged children situated in Colombia with homes caring for over three thousand children.

Again I was blessed to have worked with another of the great Catholic evangelizers of the Americas.

After Rome I returned to Canada.

HANS KUNG.

Sometime in 1985 Hans Kung, Swiss priest and theologian visited the University of Calgary.

This man had fifteen Honorary Doctorates and had received no less than fifteen Awards and Honours. He had served as theology advisor to Vatican 11, had written no less than 36 books, theological, philosophical, spiritual and on the environment.

At the time he was undergoing questioning by the Vatican, on several issues on which he had written about, such as the Infallibility of the Pope and therefore the Vatican, he was not supportive of John Paul 11 whom the Church later Canonized.

In 1979 he had been stripped of his license to teach as a Catholic Theologian.

However I had read so much about this brilliant man I could not miss his visit and I had to go and listen to him.

Although de-barred from teaching in Catholic Institutions he remained a Catholic Priest until his death in 2021.

The lecture was supposed to take place at the Calgary University's great hall, but there were so many people insisting to listen to him, without tickets, that the organizers had to make a change of plan. There was a large Auditorium close bye so the lecture was shifted to that place. Those of us with tickets would have first choice of seating place. I got myself nicely seated close to the podium.

His choice of topic was naturally non-controversial and so he dealt with what he called "Paradigm Change In The History of Theology and Church".

He dealt with the subject the 1st Century Judeo-Christianity, or rather the Primitive Church going through the different stages of Church development from early to medieval through the Protestant Reformation to contemporary Christianity through Liberation theology. Touching on the works of Origin, Augustine, Thomas Aquinas, Luther/Calvin/ Schleiermacker and of course Ratzinger (Pope Benedict XV1)

Father John Bertulluci: The *Glory of God* TV Programme

From San Diego I went to Dallas, Texas, to meet with the staff of in the headquarters where the FACE group produced their TV programme the *Glory of God*.

Joe with Father Diego Jaramillo and Toni and Terri Desoiza of the Glory of God *community.*

I met with Father Diego Jaramillo in Rome in 1984, when he was president of the Catholic Charismatic Renewal Movement.

He was with his technical team, who produced a popular Catholic TV programme for the United States. The broadcast was recorded in English language, narrated by Father John Bertolluci, whom I had befriended at Steubenville University.

My objective was to arrange with them a series of programmes to be transmitted to Canada We went through the choices I had and decided I would a city situated on the other side of the Rio Grande at El Paso.

At El Paso, another group, the Lord's Ranch, had another outreach program. Its spiritual director was Father John Scanlan, a Franciscan priest, and Principal of Steubenville University.

The Lord's Ranch had been conceived by a prayer group in El Paso who had been donated a huge section of land where they grew a variety of produce which they transported on a regular basis to the impoverished town of Juarez, across the river in Mexico. I was able to visit the ranch and see for myself the wonderful outreach they had created.

The first TV series I was to broadcast in Canada was about this outreach. The outreach grew because of a wonderful miracle. This programme was titled, "The Miracle at Juarez".

The story went that close to Christmas in 1982, the Prayer in El Paso was reading the passage in Luke 14:12:

> Whenever you give a lunch or dinner, do not invite your friends or brothers or relatives or wealthy neighbours. They might invite you in return and thus repay you. No, when you have a reception, invite the beggars, the crippled, the lame and the blind. You should be pleased that they cannot repay you, for you will be paid in the resurrection of the just.

When the time came for the group to meditate on this passage, they resolved that on the next approaching Christmas, the members would forsake their Christmas lunches and dinners. Instead, they would all go across the border to Juarez, known for having several districts of destitute people in horrendous living conditions. This was particularly true where the garbage was dumped, and children of all ages went there to scavenge whatever and thereby make some kind of living.

On Christmas Day the group members loaded their cars and a couple of trucks with an assortment of food. They calculated that they carried enough food to distribute to a couple hundred people. Apples, oranges, bread, potatoes, carrots, sugar-turnips, milk, sugar, flour, sliced ham, and so on.

The cars and trucks entered the notoriously poor district and set up shop. On hearing what was happening, people from the neighbourhood started together. The team carefully distributed its merchandise. The distribution went on for hours. When there were no longer people waiting to get their share of the food, the team was astonished to see how much food they had left over. So much that they decided to distribute it to a nearby residence for the elderly.

When they crossed the border back to El Paso, exhausted, they wondered what had really happened. They realized that they had distributed to well over a thousand persons, and that there was still food left over for the elderly residence. How could this be? They concluded that it was like the miracle that accompanied Jesus when He distributed bread and fishes to the masses on the hill:

> "Jesus' words to his disciples were: There is no need for them to disperse. Give them something to eat yourself." "We have nothing here," the disciples replied, "But only five loafs and a couple of fish."

> "Bring them here he said." He took the five loafs and the two fish, looked up to heaven, blesses and broke them and gave the loaves to the disciples, who in turn gave it to the people.

> A large mass of followers had been fed, and what was left filled twelve baskets.

This very night, on Christmas Day in Juarez, this miracle had been replicated in modern times. All those present ate their fill. The distributing team from El Paso delivered what had been leftover to the residence of elderly persons in the area.

Was this Juarez event another miracle like the multiplication of the bread on the Mount?

At Steubenville University

Steubenville University Chapel

In 1984 and 1985 I visited Steubenville University in Philadelphia to participate in a week-long summer study course on scripture. This university was run by Franciscan priests and laypeople and was considered a Charismatic Renewal institution.

In 1985 the brilliant scripture scholar Fr Herbert Sneider SJ, of German origin, took us through a line-by-line study of the Book of Revelation. In 1985 he again gave us a line-by-line study on the Gospel of Luke.

After dinner, all the participants met at the University's chapel to pray. When prayer was over at the chapel, a group of co-participants and I went up to my room, a single bed bedroom. It was an amazing experience for over fifteen people gathered, in my small bedroom, to continue to pray and share scripture.

Joe presenting his painting of the Holy Trinity to Fathers Herbert Sneider and John Bertulluci at Steubenville University

At the start of the Conference I made friends with a couple from Texas. We shared many lunches and dinners together, talking about all kinds of topics. The lady dragged on leg and walked with a limp due to a metal leg brace, she needed to wear because of a muscular problem she had for years. During one of the prayer sessions in my bedroom, we heard someone cry out in loud exclamation, "Oh!" We turned to find out who it was; it was the lady with the iron brace. Only the brace was no longer on her leg. She was holding it up in the air. She claimed that as we prayed, she felt a hot sensation on her leg. She reached down to remove the brace, thinking that it was creating a pressure point around her leg. When she took it off, the pressure and hot sensation went away, and she realized that she was standing firmly on both legs. The ailing leg she had suffered with for so many years had recovered its strength. The room went up in an uproar of praises and tears. We had experienced a miracle in our midst.

Joe addressing the hundred-strong participants at the University of Steubenville, 1985

During these periods I also met with two other priests who were great personalities in the United States— Father John Bertolluci, a well-known itinerant preacher and teacher, and Father Michael Scanlan TOR, who was president of the Steubenville University and initiated a series of major reforms to restore the school to its Catholic heritage. The school changed its name to the University of Steubenville on achieving university status in 1980. It adopted its current name, Franciscan University of Steubenville, in 1986.

I tried to arrange a meeting with Fr. John but I was told that he had a full agenda, disappointed I continued with the day's activities. When I returned to my room I found a note pinned to my door, it said "Fr. John has had a cancellation and would gladly see you at 8p.m. tomorrow evening at the Library.

So promptly I went to the Library.

First of all I asked Fr. John to hear my confession and then I mentioned to him the real purpose for my visit with him.

I proposed to Fr. John to come to Calgary, Canada and be guest speaker at a Catholic Charismatic Conference I had previously discussed with the Renewal's Core-Group in Calgary.

Fr. John agreed to come to Calgary. The meeting was scheduled for June the 15th 1986, at the JUBILEE AUDITORIUM, CALGARY with a seating capacity of 2,500.

Calgary had a population of around 1 million and was composed of 68 Catholic parishes with a Catholic population of 400,000 certainly an audience worth aiming for. The Auditorium was almost full and the Conference turned out to be a huge success.

I broke the ice by addressing the audience first, to give a short testimony of my newly found faith and then encouraged them to support the forthcoming T.V. Programme "THE GLORY OF GOD".

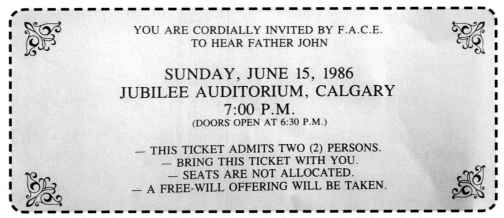

YOU ARE CORDIALLY INVITED BY F.A.C.E.
TO HEAR FATHER JOHN

SUNDAY, JUNE 15, 1986
JUBILEE AUDITORIUM, CALGARY
7:00 P.M.
(DOORS OPEN AT 6:30 P.M.)

— THIS TICKET ADMITS TWO (2) PERSONS.
— BRING THIS TICKET WITH YOU.
— SEATS ARE NOT ALLOCATED.
— A FREE-WILL OFFERING WILL BE TAKEN.

Invitation to Fr. John Bertulluci's talk on the "GLORY OF GOD" T.V. programme.

I then introduced Father John and he proceeded to deliver one of his powerful sermons/come teaching titled *"God has visited his people"*.

That night many persons answered the Alter Call for prayers and more came forward to support the T.V. programme.

Also during the Institute I did a painting of the Holy Trinity which I proposed to present, at the end of the Institute, to both Frs. Herbert Snieder and John Bertulluci since they had been the two main teachers at this Institute, on behalf of the over one hundred participants who had taken part in the Institute. On presenting the painting I said: "Holy Trinity, we praise you and thank you for giving Steubenville to the world.

We ask you, Blessed Trinity, to anoint all these good people who in accordance with Y your last command to go and spread "THE GOOD NEWS" throughout the World.

May, God Bless and protect all these messengers and servants in this noble and glorious Task."

Father Michael Scanlan T.O.R., was the founder and leader of FACE, the Franciscan Association for Catholic Evangelization, who were the promoter of the popular US TV programme titled the *Glory of God*, which I intended to sponsor and air in Calgary.

The programme had the potential of reaching over 1.2 million households in Canada and Seattle areas.

Canadian law required TV broadcasts to include at least 10 per cent Canadian content. This presented a problem because the programme was produced in the United States. We gave some thought to this and arrived at a solution. We would include the 10 per cent Canadian content by producing our own introduction to each series. A local Calgary TV station agreed to help with the production of this since we would be buying half-hour broadcast time in their station every Sunday.

The next day a mobile transmitting T.V. vehicle parked in the front of my house. Cables were laid, and the camera started rolling.

My beautiful sitting room with lovely brown velvet and lace curtains, brass ornaments, Spanish antique captain's cabinet and ornate bookshelf became the location for the recording of the "introduction" of the *'Glory of God' weekly* series the first of thirteen episodes.

I and another member of the Charismatic Renewal Prayer Group, we introduced the programme which would be split at the beginning of the original video to be broadcast at 7 a.m. every Sunday for the next three months.

First feed-back on the first Series of the *'Glory of God'*.

The night of the day the episode was shown a lady called. She had watched the programme; she was a lapsed Catholic, had lost all her loved ones and thought there was no God and that there was no purpose to life.

She said that as soon as the programme was ended she got up, dressed and went to her Church. She attended Mass and received Communion. She told me that the programme had touched her so much that her faith had returned and that she now felt a changed person.

Cristo Rey Prayer Group

Cristo Rey Prayer Group, Calgary, 1985

In the mid-1980s, many countries in Central America were undergoing political unrest. These included Guatemala, Honduras, Nicaragua, and El Salvador. These political disturbances produced tremendous conditions when hordes people immigrated to Canada, escaping as political refugees from these countries.

Calgary was one of those prosperous Canadian cities which drew thousands of Spanish-speaking refugees. Many turned to the Catholic churches for help with for a variety of reasons including clothing, food, work, and moral support. For these Catholics, the church was a place of primary support.

Since I spoke Spanish, I was approached by various parishes to give a hand in helping the many other Canadian volunteers who were giving of their time, money, clothing, and foodstuff.

But because I was very busy with my business, I at first refused to help. But then I thought that the best way I could help these people was to get them together in the form of a church group. In fact, a Charismatic Prayer group in which they could share their experiences, form friendships, and pray together. Spiritual support was as important as material help.

I started calling people on a long list I had been given and asked them to come and meet. When the group finally came together, we decided to call it *Grupo Cristo Rey*. The group grew to about fifty persons.

Several members were schoolteachers who told us that they had experienced firsthand the massacre of many of their fellow teachers, male and female alike. Some faced the imprisonment of family members who then disappeared from the face of the earth. It was a horrendous and sad history of that part of the world, where brutality and fanaticism had taken their toll. Words could not describe the heart-wrenching stories that we heard from these eyewitnesses who escaped persecution by a miracle.

When I arrived in Gibraltar in 1987 and did the rounds of the Charismatic Prayer groups, I realized that all the groups there were held in the Spanish language. And though I had led a Hispanic prayer group, I felt an urge to go to an English-speaking prayer meeting. A couple of other persons held the same view as I did. One was Charles Harrison, a great prayer warrior, and the other was John Byrne a committed Christian.

The three of us got together and started a new English-speaking Prayer Group. I had spoken to them about the Cristo Rey Prayer Group, which I had lead in Calgary, and coincidentally the new English-speaking group was called, Christ the King.

The Lady on the Plane

It was on my flight back to Canada. I settled in my seat, brought out my bible and started to read whilst the aircraft prepared to take off. From the corner of my eye I observed a lady across the aisle being asked to move from her seat; she was in the wrong seat. A few minutes later I noticed she was again being asked to move. This time she was directed to the window seat next to me.

She was quite taken by the fact that I was reading the bible and started chatting with me. Her name was Margaret. She told me, "I must say that it is not often you see someone reading the Bible." I asked if she were going on holiday, and she explained that she was travelling to Calgary because her son's wife had just died. She had apparently been diagnosed three months ago with cancer which turned out to be terminal.

I felt awkward. There was I, with a Bible in my hand, and words failed me. "I am terribly sorry for your loss," I tried to say. But she did not let me finish as she had more to say. She had left her husband behind and alone in Halifax because of another grave situation. Their other son and a friend had gone on a fishing trip three days ago and had failed to return. They were missing and feared drowned. God, please help me, I prayed silently, I don't know what to do or say. Finally, I held my bible and said, "Listen, Margaret, this must be terrible for you, and words fail me. But may I ask you to pray with me? But let's not pray for the dead. Let's pray for the living and that God may give you all the strength and courage to see this tragedy through."

We talked and prayed together for the duration of the flight. Tears often came to her eyes. When the plane got to Calgary six hours later, with teary eyes we said goodbye and parted. As I waited to collect my luggage, a young man approached me and asked me if I was Joe. I said yes. "I am Margaret's son," he said. "I want to thank you for keeping my mum company during the flight. This is the first time she has ever flown."

I thought he was going to thank me for the praying and the Bible sharing, but when he added it was Margaret's first flight apparently our praying had served to keep her mind off the flight. Frankly I did not expect this, but they say that God works in mysterious ways. Well who knows?

On Another Flight

On a flight from Denver to Calgary, I settled into my seat. And as was my custom, I brought out my worn pocket bible and started to read. One could ask, "How many people read a bible during a flight?" Well that thought came to my mind, and I figured very a few. But I was proven wrong!

When relaxed, put my bible down, and looked around me. You could have knocked me over with a feather. All the passengers to my right and left, and those in the rows in front and behind me were all reading their bibles! It happened that I was sharing a flight with members of a Mormon on their way to a convention.

Sharing Hurts: A Visit to Lourdes

Later I made a business trip to Brussels in Belgium and then on my return I had a stopover in Gibraltar. I managed to get a seat on a trip go to go to Lourdes with my brother Charles who was then Gibraltar's Vicar General Charles.

On the flight there I sat next to an old friend from my technical college days, Charles Perera, and his wife, Mari. They were with another couple, Albert Martinez and his wife. One couldn't wish to meet nicer people.

In Lourdes we kept each other company and went to various services together. We shared and prayed together and found great solace in each other.

Charles and Mari's daughter had fallen victim to leukaemia and consequently died at a very young age. It was a tremendous blow to them; their sadness and grief were deep. Only their faith kept them sane. They had lost a dear daughter in the prime of her life. Charles and Mari worked tirelessly for many years raising funds for the Leukaemia Society.

They came to Lourdes because that holy place gave them inner peace.

Albert's son had met a more tragic death, also at a young age. Their sorrow was never-ending. As God would have it, these people had met under tragic circumstances at the Chapel of Rest, both funerals having taken place on the same day. They became friends and shared their grief. Now they shared special moments together in this Holy place.

I too was mourning, I was mourning about my marriage break-up.

We all came to Lourdes seeking some kind of healing and we had found it in each other

Peace of heart and fellowship. I was grateful that God used me in some small way to be with these people at that particular time.

I, too, was in need of healing, and the examples of these folks made me realize that my problems were far from those of these kind people who accepted their tragedies with utter and complete resignation. This is the wonderful way in which God operates.

Exodus House, Calgary: A Home for Teenage Prostitutes

Fraternity House of Brothers and Sisters in Christ, Calgary, Alberta, Canada

Whilst at Lourdes I told Charles and Albert about the work I was involved in at a place called Exodus House in Calgary, Alberta, Canada. It had been set up by a group of men who rented a house owned by the local Catholic Diocese which they had converted into the Fraternity House of a Franciscan lay order called Brothers and Sisters of Christ.

When my marriage broke up, I went to live at that Fraternity House. The drastic social change for me was immense and a culture shock to my system. I was used to living in a spacious house in one of the best districts in Calgary, four bedrooms, two-car garage and situated on a beautiful and peaceful ridge with a Jacuzzi, and a live-in maid, Antonia, who looked after our very young grandson, Richard.

Girls from Exodus on a winter outing

In another property close to the Fraternity House they had started a Rehabilitation Centre called Exodus House where they tried to help teenage girls that for various reasons had taken up prostitution. The House cared for sixteen girls plus the women carers who acted as companions to the girls.

The location of the House was not made public but kept anonymous in order to keep away unwanted possible harassers.

The House ran a strict programme based on the twelve steps of Alcoholics Anonymous. This was the second time in that same year that I had encountered the AA programme.

For the first time in my life I read the organization's *Twelve Steps programme, which I found extremely spiritual, and the Twelve Traditions of AA.*

I kept asking myself what God was trying to tell me. I was baffled, but God knew better. Only time revealed God's reasons.

I was still fully employed as President of two very active businesses, so at first I did what I could as a helper of Exodus House.

All these girls had taken to the streets at an early age. Some were as young as fourteen; none were older than seventeen. Most were drug addicts, and a number were single parents.

We from Exodus House would go to Calgary's red district to East of 3rd and 4th Avenue. We tried to spot the newcomers from the dozens of seasoned ladies lining and walking the streets.

The horrendous stories these girls recounted of sexual and physical abuse, mostly by close relatives, would fill another book. Working at Exodus House was not only an eye-opener. I believe that God was preparing me for something else, though at the time, I did not know what.

I learned a lot about the subject of addiction and prostitution, but at the same time I also gained a lot of respect for women caught in prostitution. I would advise anyone not to judge prostitutes until they learn the facts and circumstances behind their lives.

It was during that period of biblical and ministerial studies and service to the community that I decided to write about the subjects of "The Power in our Hands, The Eucharist, and Heresies and the early Fathers of the Church.

I started writing because I thought that in this way, we could understand the many difficulties the Apostolic Catholic Church went through during the earlier centuries and the Middle Ages. I singled out in my writing those who fought for the Church survival to the twenty-first-century and, God willing, till eternity.

The Leper Clinic, Trinidad and Tobago: Christ Encounters Broken Bodies

Joe with Bishop McKinney and Myote Connors with lepers at a House of Light Mass

Brothers Moses and Joe singing Mass at a leper clinic

In 1985 I visited the beautiful Caribbean islands of Trinidad and Tobago, a pair of tropical islands full of colour and friendly people.

I had got in touch with Babsie Beasdle, a Catholic preacher I'd met some time earlier when she visited Canada on a preaching tour. She was very short and rather stout lady, who exuded an incredible amount of charisma. She was joyful with a permanent smile, very spiritual, and a powerfully gifted preacher.

I came to the Caribbean to attend a Caribbean Charismatic Renewal conference in Trinidad. Babsie kindly invited me to stay at her Community House in Port-of-Spain, the Ave Maria Community. The Ave Maria Community House was alive with spirit-filled young men and women. It was a hive of goodness, prayer, and charity. Their Outreach, providing food and clothing to the community.

Joe at Prayer Meeting with "AVE MARIA COMMUNIITY", TRINIDAD AND TOBAGO.

I shall never forget my first night in Trinidad. It had the distinction of being the noisiest place in the Caribbean at night. And on that first night, it seemed that hundreds of dogs from all over the city had agreed to join together in a chorus of barking, they barked incessantly all night long. It was a nightmare for this newcomer to the Island. .

On the following day five Bishops attended the conference. The Bishop of Trinidad and Tobago. Another was Bishop McKinney from the United States, known in the USA as the "Shepherd of Renewal," he was also the keynote speaker. The other Bishops were from Jamaica and from Aruba of the Dutch Antilles.

Over three thousand people were in attendance. The coloured people of the Caribbean are known for their happy and joyful natures, and during this conference, they excelled in their bubbliest friendliness.

During the celebration of the Eucharist, particularly in the silence at the moment of the blessing of the bread and wine, I noticed the people in the assembly were immersed in devotion to the point that many were in tears.

Then something happened that only people immersed in the spiritual ways of the Pentecostal drive can understand.

Someone in the congregation said, "I see Jesus. His face is full of compassion and love. His body is emaciated. He moves around us row by row; he stops by each one of us. With His wounded and cupped hands He collects the tears from each one of us. His body is frail and transparent. I can see his heart beating, and the blood flowing in His veins seems weak. He is ailing."

The man's face became radiant as people wept and sung, "Holy, Holy, Heaven and earth are full of Your glory, Hosanna in the highest."

The man continued, "Jesus returns to the assembly. Between His thumb and index fingers He holds a bright and sparkling object. He is returning to each of us the tear he took from them earlier, but these are not watery tears; they seem like sparkling diamonds. Jesus is saying, 'This is in return, for your faithfulness in coming in aid of my sick body.'"

I took this to mean that He was relying on our faith to revive His Church, His body. We were the strength remaining in His heart.

By His body, he meant His "ailing Church. Jesus was asking us, His followers, to help Him heal His Church And the reward would be great. Just like it happened to St Francis of Assisi when he was praying in the presence of an icon of the crucified Christ and heard a voice telling him, "Francis, rebuild my house, which is falling into ruin." At the time Francis di Bernardone thought God wanted him to repair the church within which he prayed. But instead, when he understood the message, he spent the rest of his life evangelizing the Good News of Jesus Christ. The diamond was the precious gift of the Holy Spirit.

At the conference Babsie introduced me to Bishop McKinney. There I also met Brother Moses, who was studying for the priesthood. Bishop McKinney had been invited to visit a special house that cared for lepers; this was located in the Island of Tobago. Babsie asked me if I minded accompanying the Bishop. I readily agreed and went along, and so did Brother Moses. We travelled to the 'House of Light' on the island of Tobago.

I shall never forget attending Mass at the House of Light.

Running the House were Mrs Myote Connors and friends, including a community of religious 'Grey Brothers of the House of Light, who had dedicated themselves to serving the most desolate, elderly, and lepers people in their district with the dedication of St. Damian of Molokai.

Three times a week volunteers collect these sick people, who have little hope of getting medical attention, and brought them to the House of Light.

The majority of patients were lepers. Some have skin diseases other than leprosy. Others are blind or lame.

If we read Leviticus 13:1–44, 46, we are told that lepers were treated as outcasts; they had to live outside the town's walls, unable to enter the temple to worship with the rest of the people, dress in rags, and cry out, "Leper, leper," as they walk the streets.

But then in, Mark 1:40–45, we read about the compassionate way Jesus dealt with the lepers who came to Him and said, "If you wish, you can make me clean," Moved with pity, He stretched his hand, touched him, and Jesus said, "I do will it. Be made clean." Jesus neither feared nor shied away from this terrible contagious disease.

In a similar way, those who volunteer at the House of Light are not afraid of caring for these and gave them medical and spiritual attention to those they served. Wounds and illnesses are washed and treated. Then they are fed a wholesome meal. And but above it all, they receive love and care.

Mass was the highlight of the day. I had the privilege of singing a couple of songs for them.

And with gusto and zest they sang, "Holy, holy, holy, God of power and might. Heaven and earth are full of Your glory. Hosanna in the highest."

We prayed the Lord's Prayer and held hands with the persons on either side of us. Strange though it felt, I thought it a privilege to hold hands with these lepers; I had Jesus in my mind.

We shared Holy Communion. "The Body of Christ", said Fr Pierre, a French missionary, as he distributed the Holy Bread. A loud, sincere, and grateful "Amen", came from the lips of every person.

I was on my knees and wondered *who is the leper or blind person here, they or I?*

When Mass was over, we heard the testimony of one of the leper patients. Most of those present suffered from leprosy, were elderly, and we could see they were suffering. Others stared emptily into space with blindness or stared into space with watery, empty eye-sockets. But one thing was evident to me: All those faces were transfigured with serenity, peace, and joy. And they were obviously very happy to be there!

I wept, not at their misfortune, but at my own wretchedness and because the love of Jesus was so real and alive in that place at that moment.

Mr Phillips (not his real name), a native of Trinidad, volunteered to give his testimony. He moved around in a wheelchair as he had lost his both his legs. His fingers bore the sign of the flesh-eating leprosy.

In his Pidgin English, Mr Phillips told us, "I was a landowner in the good old days of sugar cane plantations." He said he had rented his land to some people. After a while it became clear to him that because of his illiteracy, his tenants planned to cheat him out of his land.

He secretly resolved to avenge himself and kill the land thieves. He told us that he bought a shotgun and laid out his plan as to how he would kill these people.

He set off in his truck, but before he could put his plan into action, he had a traffic accident and lost his legs.

Mr Phillips, with a smile on his face, told us, "That was the best thing that happened to me." He dreaded the thought of his punishment, to have lost Jesus as his friend, had he murdered these people.

Mr Phillips sang with the rest of us with joy in his heart. My tears drops fell upon my guitar as I played.

As Mass finished, I looked around at those faces, still transfigured with serenity, peace, and joy! What greater manifestation could there be?

I continued to weep for the privilege of sharing the Eucharist in this distinguished Christian community.

After Mass we sat down for lunch around a huge table. Again I counted myself fortunate at the privilege of sharing the same cutlery and dishes as my leper hosts.

The love and joy of Christ was so alive and real among these people as we went about shaking hands and hugging each other saying goodbye. When it came to hugging and shaking hands with my friendly leper-friends, it was more than a compulsive desire to hug them with a brotherly Christian embrace. Such is the power of the glory of God when we share in His body.

Back In Canada.

I integrated well with the Charismatic group. And now I was not only going to Sunday Mass and weekly prayer meetings. Several weeks later I was invited to a breakfast prayer meeting that was held at the Marriot Hotel in Calgary, Canada. I had been invited to form part of the Intercession team who would stand in front of the podium and lay hands on and pray for those who came forward for prayer.

When the breakfast was over, a senior person in attendance gave a teaching from a Bible passage. After the teaching came some praise singing. Then people started coming forward for the altar call. They stood in a line in front of me. I placed my hands over their heads and prayed. I witnessed these individuals, with prayerful and peaceful smiles on their faces; go into a state of what is called "resting in the spirit", a peaceful, tranquil state. Some swayed, and with a gentle tremor, their knees slackened and they fell gently to the floor. Others standing close by caught them as they fell and safely allowed them to lie peacefully on the floor.

As the praying went on, I felt unusual warmth spreading through the palms of my hands. And when people approached for the imposition of hands, the warmth slowly increased from warm to very warm, almost hot. I was amazed and filled with a mixture of wonder and disbelief at this happening. It was happening to me to the point that I questioned how God could allow this to happen through my unworthy intervention. It made me feel very humble and inadequate, but it also made me think about the power that flows through the hands of normal men and women, allowing them to do the work for God and helping them to grow in their faith.

I continued to be invited to many prayer meetings held in the Catholic Diocese in Calgary and the surrounding towns and cities. I also attended a very successful monthly prayer meeting for businessmen held in Calgary. I soon found out that businessmen breakfast prayer meetings were held in almost every great city in Canada and the United States. This was an exciting revelation.

At a different breakfast prayer meeting held in Calgary, I was asked to join its intercessory group. After breakfast was over, a short address was given by an invited guest, who ended his talk by asking those who needed prayers to come forward.

I took my place in the front line with about six other persons. The music played, and the guest speaker invited people to walk forward. A line formed in front of me. As I prayed over the persons who came to be prayed over, I got the same warm sensation in my hands. It was such a powerful sensation that I was actually overcome by this wondrous feeling of what I would like to think was an anointing. It got so strong that I felt I had to leave the premises and go out to the garden to sit and compose myself since I felt so humble.

President Barack Obama and Prime Minister Tony Blair attended one of these businessmen's prayer meetings in the United States at the same time.

When Obama's time came to speak, he said, among many other things:

"Faith is the great cure for fear." At the same prayer breakfast, Blair, after ten years as Prime Minister, said in his presentation,

"There are many frustrations—that is evident. There is also one blessing. I spend much of my time in the Holy Land and in the Holy City. The other evening I climbed to the top of Notre Dame in Jerusalem. You look left and see the Garden of Gethsemane. You look right and see where the Last Supper was held. Straight ahead lays Golgotha. In the distance is where King David was crowned and still further where Abraham was laid to rest. And of course in the centre of Jerusalem is the Al Aqsa Mosque, where according to the Qur'an, the Prophet was transported to commune with the prophets of the past. Rich in conflict, it is also sublime in history. The other month in Jericho, I visited the Mount of Temptation. I think they bring all the political leaders there. My guide —a Palestinian—was bemoaning the travails of his nation. Suddenly he stopped, looked heavenwards, and said, "Moses, Jesus, Mohammed: why did they all have to come here?"'

I was familiar with what the marvellous works the Disciples of Jesus had gone through in the Acts of the Apostles. But this was the twenty-first century, certainly not the days of the Apostles.

Yet throughout the ages, as shown in the writings of both the Old and the New Testaments, God's love for humankind uses the hands and the mouths of sinful men and women to carry out His work of salvation on this earth. Simply because with His incarnation He brought with Him heaven to this earth of ours'.

As is evidenced in the Hebrew Bible, ordinary men and women—such as Abraham, Moses, Isaiah, and Zachariah—others become God's currency or instruments, initiating people to meet God in everyday ordinary life. As the song says, "Make me a channel of your love." He makes people currencies and vehicles for His good news. In this way, people can find God through you and me.

The Church does not depend solely on my efforts but on the unwarranted power that God, through His Holy Spirit, desires to give to His messengers; that is, you and me.

Therefore, in gratitude for everything that the Lord has done in my life, I borrow some of Mother Mary's words from the Magnificat: "My soul magnifies the Lord and my spirit rejoices in God my Saviour for he has done great things for me and Holy is His name" (Luke 1:46–49).

The Miracle of Little Melissa

One evening at the regular praying meeting at my parish church time came for participating persons to ask for intercessions if they so wished.

A lady stood up and said she needed help with her young daughter, Melissa, who had a physical problem. My mind was somewhere else, and I did not understand what the lady was going on about.

When the prayer meeting ended and people were either leaving or having a cup of coffee, I noticed that this lady was still sitting in the hall, alone and crying. I approached her and asked, "Excuse me, ma'am. Are you OK?"

Sobbing she said, "Well, I made an appeal for help, and here I am. No one has come to offer me some help."

I was tongue-tied. She was right. Here was a church hall full of Christians, and a person in need had been overlooked. I was ashamed at this lack of sensitivity by a Christian congregation.

I finally ventured to say, "Listen, *Madame why don't you give me your details and II will arrange to come and visit you and yo*ur husband, and you can then fill me in on the problem you have."

The next day I called and went to visit her and her husband. They explained that the child's disability was called, as I understood it, "Domingato?" It prevented her from learning how to crawl and, therefore, walk. This action of crawling, in Spanish is called, *gateando*, meaning crawling, cat or '*gato*', crawling was something Melissa had not done, so she had to be taught how to crawl.

The child needed five people to achieve this therapy. They moved her limbs as if swimming the crawl. This had to be done for one hour three times a day! This sounded like mission impossible to me, a big, big challenge; fifteen people were needed each day for the three one-hour sessions. This meant that 105 people were needed for the week! I wished I had not volunteered to help.

I was scheduled to go away on a ten-day business trip to the United States. But before leaving, I attended two prayer meetings. One was a ladies' prayer meeting at a nearby parish and the other at the Calgary

JOE L. CARUANA, MBE, GMD

University's chapel. When my time came to share at both prayer meetings, I mentioned the regrettable incident and how poor we were at coming forward as Christians; the spirit of the Good Samaritan somehow had failed in our church. I mentioned Melissa's case at both events leaving the family's telephone number with the leaders there. And as I left the university, I also left the family's number on a notice board with details, "Volunteers to help young girl with mobility problem". I got the feeling that I was a farmer walking his barrowed field scattering seeds as I walked. Will the seeds take hold?

I left on my business trip, but I could not get Melissa off my mind. Nor could I forget the joyful attitudes of her parents despite their very difficult circumstances. Yet there I was in the States, miles away and not being able to do anything for them. Where would I find a hundred volunteers?

"God," I prayed, "I trust I have not raised these people's hopes too high. God, give me some inspiration."

A joyful mother received me on my return. As she opened the door, she gave me a hug. "Come in, come in, Joe. How wonderful to see you. How did you do it? We are so grateful."

Utterly confused, I asked, "Do what? I have done nothing; I've been away. What are you on about?"

"Done nothing?" The mother replied. "Well one afternoon we answered the door to find a whole bunch of university students standing there. They said they had come to help Melissa and that Joe had asked them to come and help! "Then on the following day, a group of ladies also came. They, too, mentioned you and said they wanted to help Melissa". With the combined help from the university students and the ladies, we've been able to plan a schedule for Melissa's therapy."

I asked in great disbelief, "What about me? Where do I fit in?"

"Sorry, fellow. You are welcome to come for coffee, but there is no room for you in the schedule," she answered. What is the moral of the story? God works even when we sleep!

The miracle, at the time, was not that Melissa walked but that so many good people volunteered to help.

Unfortunately, when all of this was happening, I left Canada to travel to Gibraltar because my father was dying. I lost touch with the family, and I am not aware of Melissa's outcome.

Farewell, Canada

God indeed works in mysterious ways. Sometimes we make decisions and try to control our plans, but God's plans are not necessarily our own. As we have said before, He is the master snooker player. He hits a ball in one direction, that ball bounces about, and hits three different-coloured balls, and the chosen ball falls into the pocket! And so it is with our lives.

It was Christmas 1986, and I was in Red Deer, Canada. It was only two months since my heart intervention had taken place. I had ended my five-year contract but had prolonged it to seven years.

Following my recovery from a severe heart attack, while lying in my hospital bed at Foothills General Hospital in Calgary, Canada in October 1986, I looked up and saw myself hooked up to so many electronic gadgets, that I thought, *'All these years of worrying about business and so much travelling, of neglecting my family only to find myself in this way? What is this all about? Life must have more meaning than this! But what?'*

This scene took me back to 1983 when I had flown to London to visit my brother Charles and saw him hooked up to all kinds of ominous contraptions in hospital' after coronary surgery.

By now my daughters knew that I was making plans to leave Canada and return to Gibraltar. While lying in the hospital bed in the recovery room, I had questioned the reason for my existence in this world. It was certainly not to spend my time travelling around the world totally immersed in my business. I realized I had become a compulsive traveller, denying precious time to my children. So I decided to dedicate my life to something new. That something would be to start a Christian Centre, a House of rest and prayer where I could help drug addicts in the Rock. The work I had done at Exodus House had been most fulfilling, the House of Light in Tobago, Babsie's Bridal's Outreach, El Paso's Lord's Ranch, Gibraltar's Soup Kitchen, all of these excellent apostolates came to mind, I realized it had a purpose.

My mind was set!

Coincidentally in April 1987 my brother, Charles, called me in Canada to tell me that our father was seriously ill and would probably not last long. He was eighty-four years old.

I thought about the occasion when I had been called in 1961 to tell me that our mother was dying. Though I rushed immediately to go to her hoping to see her alive, I did arrived on the day of my mother's funeral, but by the time I arrived she had already been buried, I did not wish to repeat this same failure, and miss my dad's last few days on this earth.

I parted with my Franciscan friends of Exodus House, packed my things. I said goodbye to my prayer group friends, who had organized a huge farewell party for me. I was greatly touched and cried a lot that night. Everyone handed me something as a keepsake. Some gave me cards, others notes of appreciation, others personal souvenirs. I still have them.

Packing to leave Canada was not a big job. I foresaw that I would need very little, so I decided to travel light. I packed some of my heavier personal belongs in a wooden crate—my skiing boots, suit, and skis; lots of books; some of my tools; photograph albums.

The only heavy thing here was my heart in leaving Canada and all those I loved so much. It was an unimaginable truly heartbreaking ordeal. The biggest load I carried was leaving behind my daughters, even though they were independent. I felt highly confused, emotionally uncertain, and that my recently repaired heart would break in half. I was embarking upon a new start in life at 46 years old.

In a way, Canada had been good to me. But I knew deep down that I could no longer stay in this wonderful country. A sorrowful and painful review of my time in Canada flashed through my mind; I tried to balance between what I had gained and what I had lost. The balance fell heavily on the side of my losses; in fact, there were too many losses. The locusts had done severe damage to my rose garden, my family.

When I shared this moment with my brother Charles, he said, "Your life, Joe, reminds me of the life of Job. It's amazing your faith is so firm. Most people give up with fewer setbacks."

What I was not aware of was that God would one day return to me all that the locusts ate.

With tremendously mixed feelings and a metaphorically and figuratively broken heart, having sold our property on the Ridge and our holiday home on the lake shore in Kelowna.

I had left Canada and my three daughters behind and headed for Gibraltar to be there with my father brother and sister Conchi before he died.

3
CHAPTER

Back Again in Gibraltar

My father always strove to bring us up as better people. He did not want us to work like he had to work handling a boat in the Bay of Gibraltar. Little did he know his efforts went further than that? He made us all good and caring people just like him and my mother had been. Both our parents were practicing Catholics, and encouraged us to continue in our faith.

They never consciously harmed anyone. In fact, the opposite was the case. As small moneylenders they had helped numerous poor families in our neighbourhood.

I remember shortly after the World War II, at 11 years of age, being sent by my mother around the neighbourhood to collect weekly payments from borrowers. She would always send me on a Friday, which was payday. I would enter every one-shilling payment into the loan book.

Even then my parents were very compassionate, since everyone could not pay their one-shilling instalment and debts, on many occasions, went s uncollected.

In the Tradition of the Good Samaritan. During the 1936 Spanish Civil War, before I was born, ma flood of Republican refugees rushed the border between Spain and Gibraltar escaping the Nationalist Franco regime. Gibraltar, always a very giving community came to par. My parents, took in two Republican Spanish families into our flat, on separate occasions,

This was no small feat since our apartment was only a two room unit.

From somewhere in my parent's example of generosity sprouted the seed inherited by me, my brother Charles and sister Conchi's charitable dedication to others.

They fed as well as clothing them. They had arrived destitute so dad had taken them to Rodney's Men's Clothing Store, in Main Street, owned by the Gabay family and clothed them all and generously fed them too, even went to the extent of finding them jobs. One of the families, the Mottas family decided to go to Tangiers so my dad paid for his trip there. My dad and mum went to visit them in Tangiers in early 1937, and the story goes that little Joe was possibly conceived then and there!

Now this giant of a small man with a great generous heart, at 84 years old was leaving us.

I looked down at him, my Phoenician, who was once as strong and solid as an oak. The man and who had zealously protected and provided for our family, particularly when there had been little work in Gibraltar and during WWII years, in the midst of the Blitz with German bombs showering over London and us, and in the cold and hungry years in a distant evacuee camp in Northern Ireland until I reached the age of 8 years.

Thank God my brother had called me in time. I was there by my father's bedside, recalling the many stories he had told us about his life in Port Said, Egypt where he had been born, and his world travels as a very young merchant-ship crewman.

When I arrived I found him in his bed. I was shocked to see him so frail; he looked ever so small. His eyes shone on seeing me, and he gave me a big smile. I gave him a kiss on his forehead and stroked his head.

"What are you doing here?" he asked.

"Well I was just passing by, and I thought I would drop in and say hello."

"How are the girls?" He always showed so much concern for my girls.

On the morning of 9 April, at around 6 a.m., Conchi, my sister, and I called Charles to hurry over. Charles lived at the cathedral, about three hundred yards from us. Dad was fast deteriorating, he was fast leaving us.

Charles rushed over to our house in Market Lane. We had immediately prepared a small table to serve as the altar to celebrate the Holy Eucharist of thanksgiving and gratitude for our father's life I thought this was in order. It could be Toni's last Mass on this earth. The next one would be in a heavenly setting with his wife, our mother Luisa, by his side.

Conchi's, son Charles, my brother Charles, and I formed that early morning's small congregation in my father's bedroom. My brother said a few prayers, consecrated the wine and hosts and then, Communion time came, and naturally Toni could not partake of the Bread so my brother wet his lips with the blessed wine, the blood of Jesus. Our dad mumbled something, and with the blood of Jesus still wet on his tongue, he swallowed, gasped and passed away.

Later I asked my brother what had he mumbled before dying and he told me Dad said, "Al Madonna, (mother of God)," in Maltese, his native tongue. Had he caught sight, a glimpse of his parents on his deathbed? According to my brother, who had witnessed countless deaths during his fifty-four years as a priest, this was a common occurrence when people expired.

"AL Madonna", or, "Mother of God," is normally a reference to Mary, the mother of Jesus, and has been a proud Maltese plea mostly in supplication. Al is the short for Ala, the Arabic name for God.

Had Dad seen Mother Mary together with his mum and/or his dad?

After Dad passed away, I picked up my guitar, strummed a few chords, and sang in a praise-song in the language of angels that started with the word *Maranatha*, "Come, Lord, come."

Camp Emmanuel - Another Spiritual Experience.

The Power of Pentecost was pushing me on.

When I arrived in Gibraltar in 1987 I went to the local Charismatic Renewal meetings, there were several of them all in Spanish.

One day having coffee with my brother a couple joined us and my brother asked them to seat with us. I knew the man Diego Fitzgerald since his family had been neighbours of ours when, after WWII, we lived in Lynches' Lane.

I met his wife Dorothy for the first time.

We started talking and soon I found out that they were the current leaders of the Cursillo de Cristiandad Movement in Gibraltar, which was very active in our Diocese. They asked me to join the Movement and soon I was an aspirant attending a long week-end Seminar.

As they got to know me and we shared some of the things I had done in Canada they asked me to come and share in some talks they regularly held on Mondays, an Ultrella they called it.

My first talk to the group of leaders was a series of three talks which I had titled "SOME TREASURES OF VATICAN II).

The group insisted I came again so I chose to give two talks on the "Book of Revelations".

The word spread around, and soon, I was asked to give some "Teachings" at the various Charismatic Prayer Meetings.

The Cross on Top of the Hill.

In 1987, in line with my determination to set up a Christian centre to help addicts, my brother, Charles, and I motored around the region close to Gibraltar seeking a suitable location for such an endeavour.

We had given thought to starting this project in Gibraltar, but there were a couple of drawbacks to this idea. First, there were no suitable places in Gibraltar since the MOD was not releasing military lands to the local government so following my Dad's death I dedicated my time to this mission, so set in my mind.

My brother Charles and I made several trips to the surrounding country side to search for a suitable place for such a venture.

In 1987 there were no many Real Estate companies to advertise properties for sale. We were told that the best places to find out about possible available properties in the countryside were in the local bars.

We visited several potential properties, and then one day we stopped for lunch at one particular bar-restaurant for lunch. The owner came to our table to get our orders and as he looked at my brother he said, "Padre Caruana what are you doing here?"

My brother looked up and recognised the owner, "Julio! Hombre what are you doing here?"

"I am the owner of this place, 'La Ponderosa', so tell me what brings you here to this corner of the world?"

My brother proceeded to tell him what we were up to.

"Well stop looking I know of a place close by for the purpose, in fact it's just behind my place, up yonder." He pointed and offered to show us the place.

We had finally found the ideal location for 'Camp Emmanuel', or 'God with us.'

The property was secluded, had ten acres of land, a stretch of level land that was partly cultivated with two orchards, one of oranges and another with pear trees. A long stretch of hilly back-yard with a stream to the North lined with tall eucalyptus trees. It also had a couple of derelict buildings; one was a 19th century stable with bedrooms on the first floor and an adjacent basic front-room. Adjacent to the house and stable was a more modern structure that had been built as a barn; this was rather large, about 20 metres long and 15 metres wide, overlooking the orchards.

The barn was co-habited by huge rats and fat snakes that survived on the rats, a challenge to come.

Eventually we found a property close to San Martin Del Tesorillo in the Montenegral area.

All kinds of possibilities came to our minds. I immediately made a deal with the current owners and purchased the property. Later we spent many exciting hours measuring and planning the future Camp Emmanuel.

There was one problem, I had the cash to buy the property but had very little to carry out the renovations. There was only one solution to this; we would have to do the work ourselves.

We made it known this project through the local media, television newspapers and spreading the idea of this Christian project through the various Prayer Meetings.

We had response from various quarters; one was the Christian Life Movement (CLM) the other the Youth for Jesus Group, both groups catered for young people but the older leaders of these groups were mostly handy individuals.

We had invited the kind and soft spoken Father to celebrate the Mass.

Since our purpose was to create a Christian camp for the rehabilitation of addicts and for young people, we thought that the first act we should do at the Camp was to celebrate was an open-air Mass.

There was a large mulberry tree in a clearing in front of the old house and barn, and we decided to celebrate the Mass under this tree. We improvised an altar with a brick support and a couple of wooden building blanks left in the rumble of the huge storage room. As Mass was being celebrated, Father Francis Little spoke: "This is the place where Good awaits. Listen, even the birds in the sky are glad to see us. They have come out to greet and join us. Can you hear their singing?"

But when indeed the time came for the Consecration, amazingly the host of birds stopped their singing and their flying there was a pregnant pause in the place, there was total silence, to bird singing, no wings flattering.

An excellent omen if there was ever one.

The cross at the top of the hill

Faith and Light group guided by Barry

Day outing for young children—picnic and games

End of rehab, and burning the wish list

My daughter Denise, visiting to do some work

We came to understand that a location in Gibraltar was too close to home. The addicts' resistance to change was right there close to them, what I called the 'pressure-cooker syndrome', work problems, family problems, pushers, enablers, wives, girlfriends; it would be more difficult for addicts to escape from their environment. A centre in your own back-yard was only a step removed from your door-way.

I registered our Charity as 'Emmanuel Pastoral Trust', though it was not in any way either financed or governed by the Catholic Church of Gibraltar.

Black and white gathering for the celebration of the first Mass.

Eventually, in the spring of 1988, I towed the caravan that I had bought in a nearby Camp Ground to the Camp. I parked it close to two fully grown fig trees; I prepared the inside of the caravan and made it a comfortable abode. There was still no running water or sewage system.

The water was no problem I carried this in 10 litre bottles for my own use.

The sewage was also no problem, there were plenty of friendly trees in the surround area.

With time both water and sewage problem was resolved, water came from our own well 4oo metres away. A small petrol water-pump and hundreds of metres of rubber hose was installed.

With a kind donation from Joe Sheriff a heavy duty electric power cable was installed from the well-house to the building itself.

A year later we had, toilets running water and electricity, the water was taken to Gibraltar tested there, it was found to be excellent water with an abundance of minerals, and we could pump enough water to irrigate the orchards, domestic consumption and to fill the swimming pool too.

For many long periods I would sleep alone in the Camp's caravan. It was a wonderful experience. To look up at the starry sky and listen to the night-time noises by the many creatures who have a nocturnal life-style.

Somehow I was not frightened with this aloneness, even though I knew the nearby areas were the abode of pretty large snakes and large rats' I had my guitar, a small radio and a few wonderful books, this was before the electricity was installed, so a gas lantern and a gas cooker were essential.

My favourite book was Thomas Kempi's, The Imitation of Christ, whose recorded conversations with God were awe-inspiring.

The Camp was secluded and hidden from sight. It sat nestled in a small valley surrounded by orange trees, some lemon trees, and a pear orchard. There was a variety of other trees, including pine and eucalyptus, as well as olives and berries of various kinds. I spotted the perfect eucalyptus tree to be cut down to serve as a huge cross at the very top of the hill at the back of the camp.

The trees provided shelter and homes for red and green finches, blackbirds, sparrows, woodpeckers, and a couple of large owls that came out at night. The place was in total neglect. Nevertheless it was a refuge for wildlife including an abundance of metre-long snakes and nine-inch long rats that had made the decrepit old building their homes, one becoming the prey of the other.

We started work on it mostly with volunteers from Gibraltar and some groups. The first was the Christian Life Movement (CLM). Peter Cummings, a member of that group and a senior nurse and tutor at St Bernard's Hospital was of tremendous help in the early days.

He and I, like two lumberjacks, set to cutting down the huge eucalyptus tree, about fourteen inches in diameter, and prepared it to be hauled up the hill, about 200 metres of a steep gradient to the top plateau.

Help came on Pentecost Sunday 1990, when around two hundred people arrived at the camp. We celebrated Pentecost Sunday Mass and the big hall was overflowing with people; over 250 Communion hosts were distributed on that day.

Whole families came to visit in private cars and even two small buses to work and picnic.

After Mass, husbands, wives, grandparents, and children all lined on both sides of the eucalyptus tree and took up the ropes that we had wound around the truck. Slowly but surely, the tree reached the top where, with the effort of the pyramid builders in Pharaoh's time, we managed to lower the tree into a deep hole we prepared beforehand.

Almost all the children took a small plastic shopping bag full of mixed sand and cement, plus bottles of water, to the top of the hill; the concrete was to be poured around the tree when it was in place.

After the CLM group came another invaluable group of friends joined us as a family group comprising the John Martinez, Finlayson, and Joe Reyes families. These, all hard working and dedicated individuals joined to help in our project of remodelling the new Camp Emmanuel. In this group we were fortunate to have a retired carpenter, Ernest and a professional plumber, an electrician, Pepe Martinez and a professional draftsman, Mario Rodriquez. We were fortunate too to have plentiful choice of handymen available.

With the donation of an old ambulance we transported a host of castaways' items such as doors, windows, plastic pipes, heavy duty tools, picks, shovels, ladders, scaffolding, lots of gardening tools, wheel barrows etc, etc. Most of these donated by the Frendo brothers who had closed down their construction company.

From the Army stores we were donated rolls and rolls of valuable barb-wire and iron posts with which we were able to re-fence the property.

Electric Supply Company, owned by Joe Sherrif, donated us with thousands of yards of heavy duty cable to supply the place with electricity; he also donated a supply distribution box together with plugs and sockets to complete the wiring installation of the buildings.

Toilets and showers came from individuals who were remodelling their houses and had heard of us.

We praised God for all these bountiful donations.

Most of the people mentioned above had jobs and mostly came on weekends, on occasions a few who were out of work came for longer.

Even with these great donations I was still unhappy about progress. There was lots of work to be done.

Some days later I was alone at the camp, trying to knock down a wall. After hammering away for half a day, I stopped tired and sweating, in dismay I looked around.

At the top of my voice, almost screaming, I asked, "Lord what in heaven's name am I doing here all alone? Is this, Lord, what you intend for me? I am to wait till next Pentecost for workers to show up?"

In almost desperation I threw the heavy mallet down, got into my car, and drove home to Gibraltar. I cleaned up and went to have something to eat.

Ninety members of the Youth for Jesus Group, 1992

I went into a restaurant close to where I lived and a couple fellows, to remain unnamed, whom I knew well, came to chat with me. I told them that I had just come from the camp and was about to eat.

One of them told me, "Well, Joe, we are about to go across the border and have some tapas. Why don't you come with us?" I decided to go with them. I hadn't had a night with the boys for a long time, so this would be a nice break. We visited a couple of eating places and had our share of tapas and wine.

Then one of them said, "Listen, I know a place where we can get the best tapas ever. Why don't we go there?" Naively I did not understand what he meant. So I went along with them. When we arrived at the place, my hair went on end. This was not a tapas bar. It was a girlie bar, a clip joint.

I asked myself should I or should I not go in with them?

I made a resolution. Hesitatingly I walked inside, where there were a lot of girls milling around in scanty dresses. I walked straight to the bar whilst the rest went to sit in private alcoves. I was confused and pondered about my predicament, my resolution was not to participate with them. Had they planned this for my benefit? Was I the target of a bad joke?

Eventually a young lady approached me and asked me to invite her for a drink. I said, "Sorry, but I cannot afford it." She said her name was Flores and asked if I was interested in her. She said she was the top girl there, and it wouldn't be very expensive.

I knew very well what she was, but I still tensed up.

Thoughts of Exodus House in Canada came to my mind. All those horrendous testimonies I had heard from those young prostitutes in Canada, invaded my mind.

She placed a hand on my arm, and I said to her, "Listen, young lady, you are not what you think you are. Do you know that in the eyes of God, you are a pure-white lily? I have worked in a house that helped young prostitutes, like you, and I know that your work is not as glamorous as you are making it out to be. Don't you know that God loves you? What has brought you to this? What did you say your name was? Flores, you said? Well you are a flower, a white lily, in God's eyes."

I got carried away and talked to her about Mary Magdalene, the Samaritan woman by the well, and the adulteress who was about to be stoned, but Jesus told the crowd, "He who is without sin let him cast the first stone." Then Jesus said to the woman, "Woman, go and sin no more."

I told Flores that that was what Jesus was telling her now. I looked around and became a little scared, some people were watching us, and Flores started to cry, thinking that any minute one of those hefty muscle-bound bouncers would come over and throw me out by the seat of my pants. They would think that I had done something to make this lady cry.

Then Flores told me about her young sister, who was only fourteen years old and was going in the same direction as she. She asked me if I could help her sister. She gave me her telephone number so that I could call her and talk to her sister as soon as possible.

I quickly said goodbye to Flores and my friends, II had overstayed my visit, called a taxi, and went straight home. I shook most of the way till I got home. It was close to 2 a.m. when I got back.

A Call From Canada.

I sat in the living room with the T.V. on, I made myself a tea. I was wide awake. I sat done when the phone rang. I picked it up, said, "Yes?"

The voice at the other end asked, "Is that Joe?" The voice had a North American accent.

"Yes, this is Joe. Who is this please?"

"It's me, Doug, Doug from Radway Bible School in Alberta."

"Doug, how great to hear from you. It's so nice to hear your voice, praise God. What a surprise. To what do I owe the pleasure of this call, Doug? It's so unexpected."

"Well Joe, we were praying this morning at the school, and we felt that the Lord was telling us that you needed help with your project in Spain. This was confirmed in prayer throughout the morning. So obedient to God's prompting, we have decided to call you."

My heart stopped beating.

"Joe, are you there, Joe?"

"Yes, Doug. I'm here. I can't believe what I'm hearing, it's such a coincidence" I recounted to him the day's events and how I had pleaded to God for help.

"Well Joe, it seems He has answered your prayer. God is always faithful to those who love Him. Here with me are about twelve students from the Radway Bible School who are prepared to come over and help you in Spain. You won't have to spend a penny. How many students to you want?"

Did he say twelve students? I can't put up twelve. What a gift, what a prompt reply to my 'shout for'!

I quickly, my mind spinning, figured out that we could only accommodate two persons by allocating them in two provisional caravans that had recently donated. A third caravan was my own living quarters.

Paul, Ferdinand, and Joe fooling around

Paul, a six-foot four-inch giant of a young man, and Ferdinand, a smaller giant at five foot six inches travelled from Canada and remained at the camp for over four months. Their spirituality and devotion to service to others were exemplary. And the amount of practical work which they carried out with so much enthusiasm was both contagious and invaluable.

But above all, both young men made an impact with the host of young people who visited the camp with their Prayer Groups.

We were so privileged that God arranged for these two young Canadian Catholic prayer-warriors to come to Camp Emmanuel.

On retrospect I thought that maybe God had put me to the test that night when I was taken to a 'Clip Joint' that night, by two friends, and I was faced with Lily the prostitute.

Those who came to the camp for treatment underwent a drug or alcohol rehabilitation recovery programme that was based on the 12-Step Alcoholics Anonymous— AA— programme also had a few hours of hands-on work.

Our two Canadian guests mingled and shared their experiences with a few of the patients we had in those early days.

During the late-1980s, there were no trained therapeutic addiction counsellors. Even doctors were not familiar with treating addiction as an illness.

Even then our patients received one–on-one counselling. Once a week volunteer Jon Searle, who had been a former therapist in Liverpool for young men, came for this sessions. Lessons on relaxation and meditation were given by Lina Searle who happened to be a professional physiotherapist. We were also provided with a weekly visit by a qualified nurse who gave talks and provided counselling on venereal diseases, when necessary. Several priests also volunteered to come to the camp to talk to the young men about their personal family problems.

Members of the Christian Life Movement-1992 Retreat

Pentecost Sunday was always a joyful occasion. It had become a yearly event at the camp, this involved young kids and their parents visiting the Camp. Over two hundred persons would come to celebrate Pentecost, to celebrate the down-pouring of the Holy Spirit upon the gathered Apostles and Mary.

We always tried to find time to invite several institutions to come and visit, for the day, persons who would enjoy a visit to the countryside and be provided with a lovely lunch, tea and always music. The service being provided mostly by volunteers and resident patients.

We invited elderly residents from Mount Alvernia, patients from the physiological KGV hospital, as well as groups from the Elderly Association, and disabled young person's residents from Doctor Giraldi's respite residence. We also organized retreats for the separated and widowed ladies. Young people's retreats of hundreds of young boys and girls came for the weekends, organized by the CLM.

We even arranged to hold a one week-long retreat for seminarians from the Cadiz Seminary. We also invited patients from Hogar Marillac, a house run by nuns in Spain, who treated both men and women with terminal HIV.

When we helped these addicts, who over the years numbered several hundred, I recalled the vision revealed in the Trinidad and Tobago Conference of the ailing body of Christ.

The Christian spirit in the Camp, by all of those who came to help at the Camp, influenced many of those who had come for help with their addictions. I humbly offered all these works to God in the hope that my church, Christ's body on earth, would grow strong with new blood.

Through the passing years we saw many of these people re-insert themselves into society, marrying and building families. What more could I ask of a loving God? In 1994 the stress I had submitted myself to took its toll, and I suffered a severe heart attack that required open-heart surgery with four bypasses.

Three months after the operation, I was back again at the camp which continued in operation until late 1998.

From the very Sunday day, when I went to Mass the near-bye town of El San MartinTesorillo, I made friends with the local recently ordained young priest, Lazaro Albar.

We became great friends and companions. He would come to help at the Camp and I would help him at his Parish.

Fr. Lazaro had 4 parishes to look after and he was also a great itinerant evangelizer, giving lectures and leading spiritual retreats in a wide neighbouring area called El Campo de Gibraltar.

He asked me if I would become a Special Minister of the Eucharist and help him celebrate the Liturgy of the Word Service, to lead the local children's choir on Sundays and help with Catechesis for children preparing for their first Communion.

I gladly assisted him on all of these and somehow found the time to do this!

Since he did not as yet drive a car I offered to drive him to many of his many commitments in other Parishes where he directed spiritual retreats and gave lectures.

It was an engrossing matter on top of my duties at the Camp directing the 12 Step recovery programme.

Seeing how keen I was on evangelization he soon asked me to give an introductory talk prior to his. He said we seemed like Paul and Silas of the Acts of the Apostles.

As time went on, I prayed on the thought of entering a Seminary to prepare myself for Holy Orders as a Priest in the Cadiz Province. I conferred with my brother on this who was fully aware of my many years of commitment to my work.

Lazaro and I compiled a dossier with a record of my spiritual work and formally presented the dossier to the Bishop of Cadiz.

I need to add that it was tradition for the clergy in the Province of Cadiz to celebrate the Easter Feast of the lamp. My brother always attended this gathering of hundreds of priest, including the Bishop of Gibraltar.

However as would happen that particular year 1992 my brother, fortunately or unfortunately could not attend the gathering which he would normally not miss.

The Bishop of Cadiz who was the host of that gathering looked for Vicar General Charles Caruana but could not find him so instead he approached the Bishop of Gibraltar directly and innocently asked the

Bishop what can you tell me about Father Caruana's application to enter the Seminary in Cadiz? My friend Lazaro with several other priests, who all knew me well, was standing there when the question was put.

They told me that the Gibraltar Bishop almost had an apoplexy episode; he went all red and blew his top. So expressive was his reaction that I was told, two months later that the Bishop of Cadiz following this adverse reaction he could not consider my application.

I have said several times above that God has a funny way of playing snooker.

Lazaro apologetically gave me the bad news and I had no recourse but to accept. I thought *"Well there must be a good reason why God has not granted my desire."*

Funnily enough I had recently read St. Paul's Letter to the Corinthians where he advised: *"A man is better off having no relations with a woman. But to avoid immorality, everyman should have his own wide and every woman her own husband."* (1 Cor. 7: 2-3)

A short time, also in a game of snooker and, round-about-way, I met a lady who happened to be separated though eventually she widowed - who after several years of courtship she became my dear, inseparable wife, Ana! A living example that God never lets you down, that when one door closes another a brighter door opens.

Joe leading the children's choir at Sunday Mass at San Martin Del Tesorillo Church

My bed was no all a bed of Roses. I must confess that around that time, even with a large group of volunteers and a long list of waiting patients for treatment, from within my own Church in Gibraltar there were some who did not appreciating the kind of work we were doing for our society at Camp Emmanuel.

Even though my brother was the Vicar General of Gibraltar his contribution to the mission was negligible and superficial, he held back from giving his full support owing to the potential criticism that invariable came from within church members themselves, who might believe that the my brother was using the Church to help me personally to make money.

There always, in a small parochial town, 'Fire-fighters' willing to put out the fire that comes from those with good intentions and there are always people willing to attribute ulterior motives to good works.

There are always, well intentioned persons, who block the way to God's works. As the saying goes, 'The way to hell is paved with good intentions'.

Since in those years I floated with the wings of the Franciscan spirit my mind was set on working in God's fields as a simple labourer. The question lay between God, me and the people that God sent my way. I thank God for this great privilege.

4
CHAPTER

The Power of Pentecost

The New Testament is full of allegories where 'hands' played a significant part, particularly early in Jesus' ministry and throughout the Acts of the Apostles. The use of hands is mentioned in the Bible for prayer, with hands in the 'Orans' position, for thanksgiving, in supplication, in praise, or in prayers for healing.

The use of hands manifesting the power of God in individuals is not exclusive to the New Testament. They are also manifested, as we will see later, in the Old Testament.

Painting found in the roman catacombs. Courtesy Wikipedia.

When in 1984 I visited the Roman catacombs,, the underground hiding place of persecuted Christians of the first and second centuries, I was shown a faded coloured fresco on the wall of one of the small chambers in a warren of underground passages and chambers. A "Beato" had been painted with his hands uplifted in prayer which illustrated clearly the way in which early Christians prayed. The painter had portrayed a vivid example of a normal prayer stance.

Knowing that the Maltese people also pray in that fashion, years later, in Gibraltar, I asked an elderly gentleman of Maltese extraction how his family and mine prayed in the old days, and he demonstrated the Orans position. Then he told me that prior to WWII and after, when the huge Royal Navy fleets came to Gibraltar, thousands of sailors from the battleships went ashore on liberty to shop and drink.

The fleet also consisted of a very large contingent of crew that were of Maltese origin. When on shore the first stop for the British sailors was the bars, and for the Maltese sailors, it was the Catholic Cathedral in Main Street. The elderly gentleman said the church would fill to capacity with the sailors in a sea of white and blue naval uniforms. He told me their chanting could be heard from, "several hundred yards away. They stood and prayed with their arms outstretched in prayer."

But not only Christians used this posture, Jews and Moslems also use the Orans posture when praying.

But why this demonstration of uplifting of hands? It will become clear as we examine the Bible for those occasions when the use of hands was prevalent.

It is written that one of these instances was when the Apostles, who were under persecution, appealed to God and prayed, "And help your servants to proclaim your message with all boldness, by 'stretching out your hand' to heal and to work miracles and marvels through the name of your holy servant Jesus" (Acts 4:30). A clear example that the laying on of hands is always accompanied by prayers.

Jesus' ministry was not all a bed of roses. During His travels He met with resistance from various quarters, least of which were the Sadducees and the Pharisees. On several occasions, particularly in His hometown of Nazareth, He was rejected by His own people, leading him to remark, "No prophet is without honour except in his native place, indeed in his own house" (Matt. 13:57).

In the opening of Luke's gospel, Luke diligently writes,

> *Forasmuch as many have taken in hand to draw up a narrative concerning those matters which have been fulfilled among us, even as they delivered them unto us, who from the beginning were eyewitnesses and ministers of the word, it seemed good to me also, having traced the course of all things accurately from the first, to write unto thee in order, most excellent Theophilus; that thou might know the certainty concerning the things wherein thou was instructed. (Luke 1:4)*

It is clear that Luke, the Greek medic, compiled his account from the accounts of the travels and works done by the Apostles. He recorded the eyewitness accounts, and possibly, letters that circulated from Jesus' Disciples and written to various churches throughout the Empire.

It is abundantly clear too, from this Gospel, that Luke was no stranger to Jewish ways and very familiar with the Torah and Jewish customs

The Power of Hands in the Old Testament.

The act of the imposition or laying on of hands appears early in the Old Testament and with varying connotations: (a) in the act of blessing (Gen. 48:14); (b) in the ritual of sacrifice where the server 'laid hands' on the head of the sacrificial animal (Exod. 29:10, 15, 19; Lev. 1:4; 3:2, 8, 13; 4:4: 24, 29; 8:14; 16:21); and (c) in witness-bearing in capital offenses and above all when conferring authority (Lev. 24:14).

In Old Testament times, sacrificing was a divine order as was the appointment of someone to the priestly order. The tribe of Levi was set apart for the priestly order by the solemn imposition of hands:

> *The Lord spoke to Moses ... While the Levites are present before the Lord; the Israelites shall 'lay their hands' upon them. Let Aaron then offer the Levites before the Lord as a wave offering from the Israelites, thus devoting them to the service of the Lord. (Num. 8:10)*

When Moses appointed Joshua to be his successor by a similar act, the Lord replied to Moses,

> *Take Joshua, son of Nun, a man of spirit 'and lay your hand upon him'. Have him stand in the presence of the priest Eleazar … Invest him with some of your dignity, that the whole Israelite community may obey him. (Num. 27:18–23)*

> *Now Joshua, son of Nun was filled with the spirit of wisdom, since Moses 'had laid his hands' upon him. (Deut. 34:9)*

The idea of the imposition of hands in these cases varies with the purposes of the acts to be performed. The primary idea seems to be that of conveyance or transference of divine power:

> *'Laying both hands', he shall confess over it all the sinful faults and transgressions of the Israelites, and so put them on the goat's head. He shall then have it led into the desert by an attendant. Since the isolated region, it must be sent away into the desert. (Lev. 16:21)*

But conjoined with this, in certain instances, are the ideas of identification and of devotion to God, even in the performance of a miracle. I immediately thought of two instances where one of God's prophets, specifically Moses, employed his hands to perform powerful miracles.

When escaping from the clutches of Pharaoh, Moses explained, "When I have gone out of the city, 'I will spread out my hands in prayer' to the Lord. The thunder will stop and there will be no more hail, so you may know that the earth is the Lord's" (Exod. 9:29).

This was an impressive use of the power of hands on the occasion when Amalek waged war against Israel at Rephidim. Moses ordered Joshua to engage the enemy and told him,

> *I will be standing on top of the hill with the staff of God in my hand … As long as Moses 'kept his hands raised up', Israel had the better of the fight, but if he let his hands rest, Amalek had the better of the fight. Moses hands however grew tired; so they put a rock in place for him to sit on. Meanwhile Aaron and Hur 'supported his hands', one on one side and one on the other, 'so that his hands remained steady till sunset'. And Joshua mowed down Amalek and his people with the edge of the sword. (Exod. 17:12–13)*

In another instance, it is written,

> Then Moses left Pharaoh and went out of the city. 'He spread out his hands' toward the Lord; the thunder and hail stopped, and the rain no longer poured down on the land. (Exod. 9:33)

We can clearly see that the anointing in Moses's hands was so powerful that even the natural elements obeyed his bidding.

The leadership of the people of Israel changed from Moses to Joshua, but only after Moses performed an act of transference of power using his hands:

> Now Joshua, son of Nun, was filled with the spirit of wisdom, since Moses 'had laid his hands upon him'; and so the Israelites gave him (Joshua) their obedience, this caring of the Lord's command to Moses. (Deut. 34:9)

Here we see the passing on of divine powers as prescribed by the Lord Himself, something we will see happening in the time of Jesus and the Apostles, when the Lord decided to spread the power of His salvation, not only on the Jews, but to all the peoples of the world.

The spilling of blood in Jewish rituals is a precursor of the bleeding sacrifice that Christ underwent once and for all for the remission of sins that enabled the merciful act of salvation for humankind. The Jews of Jesus' time could easily identify with the words of sacrifice that Jesus employed at the Last Supper:

> All of you must drink from it, for this is my blood of the covenant, to be poured out in behalf of many for the forgiveness of sins. (Matt. 26:27, 28)

> When he had brought forward the bullock for a sin offering, Aaron and his sons 'laid their hands 'on its head. Then Moses slaughtered it, and taking some of its blood, with his fingers he put it on its horns around the altar, thus purifying the altar. He also made atonement for the altar by pouring out the blood at its base when he consecrated it. (Lev. 8:14–15)

After Moses called Aaron forward, dressed him in the priestly garments as ordered by the Lord, and ordaining Aaron and his sons as priests, the scriptures say:

> On the eighth day Moses summoned Aaron and his sons to give up a ram for holocaust … Aaron 'then raised his hands over the people and blessed them'. When he came down from offering the sin offering and holocaust and peace offering, Moses and Aaron went into the meeting tent. On coming out they again blessed the people. The glory of the Lord was revealed to all the people. Fire came forth from the Lord's presence and consumed the holocaust and the remnants of the fat on the altar. Seeing this, all the people cried out and fell prostrate. (Lev. 9:22–24)

It appears that the number of life sacrifices carried out on the ritual altar was regular and frequent:

> When he has completed the atonement rite for the sanctuary, the meeting tent and the altar, Aaron shall bring forward the live goat. 'Laying both his hands on its head', he shall confess over it all the sinful faults and transgressions of the Israelites, and so put them on the goat's head. (Lev. 16:21–22)

In the first sacrifice we read that the bullock was sacrificed. But in the second instance, the goat, which bore all the transgressions and sinful faults of the Israelites on its head, was not sacrificed. Instead it was taken out to the distant desert and we assume was left to perish there, far from the people.

Here again, in these sacrifices, we see a foreshadowing of Jesus' sacrifice and shedding of blood for the transgressions of humankind with the promise of the forgiveness of sins. . After Jesus' sacrifice on the cross, it was no longer necessary to sacrifice animals, since Jesus as the Lamb of God had undergone the ultimate sacrifice:

The Lord said to Moses:

> Speak to Aaron and his sons and tell them: This is how you shall bless the Israelites. Say to them: "The Lord bless you and keep you! The Lord let his face shine upon you, and be gracious to you! The Lord looks upon you kindly and give you peace! So shall they invoke my name upon the Israelites, and I will bless them." (Num. 6:22–27)

Probably the most beautiful blessing of all times, a blessing perpetuated by St Francis of Assisi.

The one who blesses is the Lord. We bless with God's blessing, not our own.

A further example of the community's authority is shown in this verse, when the people acknowledge and impart the communal power of the priesthood through the laying of hands: "When you present the Levites before the Lord, the people of Israel must lay their hands on them" (Num. 8:10).

And,

> The Lord said to Moses, take Joshua, son of Nun, a man of spirit and 'lay your hand upon him'. Have him stand in the presence of the priest Eleazar and of the whole community, and commission him before their eyes. Invest him with some of your own dignity, that the whole Israelite community may obey him. (Num. 27:15–23)

This laying on of hands can be seen as one of empowerment:

> Then Joshua, son of Nun, was filled with the spirit of wisdom, since Moses had 'laid his hands upon him' and so the Israelites gave him their obedience, thus carrying out the Lord's. (Num. 27:15–25)

> "Then at the time of the evening sacrifice, I rose in my wretchedness fell on my knees, 'stretching out my hands' to the Lord, my God. God, for our wicked deeds are heaped up above our heads and our guilt reaches up to heaven." (Ezra. 9. 5-6)

> Here is an instance where hands accompanied a confession and contrition.

> A man chosen by God, Isaiah's lips were purified with a life coal from the altar. He became known as the "Messianic Prophet" because it was he who presaged all that Jesus would have to endure in fulfilment of his prophecies concerning the Messiah who was to come. Isaiah had a vision concerning the ways of Judah and Jerusalem, and he recounted a long list of grievances which the Lord had against them (the Israelites). And through Isaiah, the Lord spoke, "Your new moons and festivals I detest; when you 'spread out your hands', I close my

eyes to you; though you pray the more I will not listen. Your hands are full of blood! Wash yourself clean!" (Isa. 1:14–15).

When Isaiah was professing the restoration of Zion by the Lord, he says:

The Lord has sworn 'by his right hand and his mighty arm': No more will I do not give your grain as food to our enemies; nor shall foreigners drink your wine for which you toiled. But you who harvest the grain shall eat it, and you shall praise the Lord; you who gather the grapes shall drink the wine in the courts of my sanctuary. (Isa. 62:8–9)

It is written that when the Lord got angry with His chosen people, He punished them thus:

They forgot the God who had saved them, who had done great deeds in Egypt, wondrous deeds in the land of Ham, terrible things at the Red Sea. Then he spoke of exterminating them, but Moses, his chosen one, withstood him in the breach to turn back his destructive wrath. Yet they despised the desirable land; they believed not his word. They murmured in their tents, and obeyed not the voice of the Lord. Then with 'raised hands' he swore against them to let them perish in the desert, to scatter their descendants among the nations, to disperse them over the lands … Yet he had regard for their affliction when he heard their cry; and for their sake he was mindful of his covenant and relented, in his abundant kindness, and he won for them compassion from all who held them captive. (Ps. 105:21–46)

David in his psalms sang these prayers to the Lord:

Come; bless the Lord, all you servants of the Lord, Who stand in the house of the Lord, during the hours of night. 'Lift up your hands' towards the sanctuary, and bless the Lord. (Ps. 134:1–2)

O Lord, to you I call; hasten to me; hearken to my voice when I call upon you. The 'lifting up of my hands', like the evening sacrifice. (Ps. 141:1–2)

The Jesus' bleeding crucified Christ was now 'The Lamb of God', it was not an empty sacrifice. After Jesus' sacrifice on the cross it was no longer necessary to sacrifice animals, since Jesus as the Lamb of God has undergone the ultimate sacrifice; "One of the elders said to me: 'Do not weep. The Lion of the tribe of Judah, the Root of David, has won the right by his victory to open the scroll with the seven seals.

Then between the throne with the four living creatures and the elders, I saw a Lamb standing, a Lamb that had been slain." (Rev.5. 5:6.NAB). This was a direct reference to Jesus.

Hands in the Life of Jesus

What qualifies men for the work of ministry is a gift from God. It is not of nature, nor is it mere natural abilities or anything acquired, like human learning, or the knowledge of languages, arts, and sciences.

It is a peculiar and distinct gift; it is dispensing the mysteries of grace to the edification of others, which is a treasure put into earthen vessels. A good minister of Christ brings forth many good things both for the delight and profit of men. And this gift, this talent, should not be hidden in the earth. It should not lie dormant and useless but should be stirred up as it may by reading, meditation, and prayer.

Paul wrote to Timothy, "Neglect not the gift that is in thee, which was given thee by prophecy, with the 'laying on of the hands' of the presbytery."

Above all this gift brought about by the empowerment by the Holy Spirit by the Holy Spirit is the gift that came on Pentecost,

During His earthly ministry, Jesus used His hands in many ways and for many reasons. I am greatly touched by two events recorded in both Mathew's and Mark's gospels, when they record, probably both referring to the same event:

People were bringing their little children to him to have him touch them, but the disciples were scolding them for this. Jesus became indignant when he noticed it and said to them, "Let the children come to me and do not hinder them. It is to just such as these that the kingdom of God belongs. I assure you that whoever does not accept the reign of God like a little child shall not take part in it." Then he embraced them and blessed them 'placing his hands on them'. (Mark 10:16; Matt. 19:13)

Jesus and His followers went down to Capernaum and into Peter's house. It is written:

> When Jesus came into Peter's house, he saw Peter's mother-in-law lying in bed with a fever. 'He touched her hand' and the fever left her, and she got up and began to wait on him.
>
> When evening came, many who were demon-possessed were brought to him, and he drove out the spirits with a word and healed all the sick. This was to fulfil what was spoken through the prophet Isaiah: "He took up our infirmities and carried our diseases." (Matt. 8:14–17)

Early in Jesus' ministry we read that the people knew of Jesus' power of healing when He imposed hands on someone since, on this occasion, a leader of the synagogue where Jesus had been teaching came to him. It is written:

> Before Jesus had finished speaking to them, a synagogue leader came up, did his reverence and said: "My daughter has just died. Please come and lay your hand on her and she will come back to life. Jesus stood up and followed him and his disciple did the same. When Jesus arrived he went in and said to them, 'Why all this commotion and wailing? The child is not dead but asleep. To the synagogue leader, the flute players and the crowd who were making a din he said, "Leave all of you. The little girl is not dead. She is asleep." At this they began to ridicule him. Then when the crowd had been put out he entered and took her by the hand, and the little girl got up. (Matt. 9:18–25)

The Gospel of Mark relates this account as follows:

> After he put them all out, he took the child's father and mother and the disciples who were with him, and went in where the child was. He took her by the hand and said to her, "Talitha koum!" (Which means little girl, I say to you, get up!'). Immediately the girl stood up and began to walk around (she was twelve years old). At this the family's astonishment knew no bounds. He enjoined them strictly not to let anyone know about it, and told them to give her something to eat. (Mark 5:40–42)

When Jesus returned to Nazareth, His hometown, He realized that the people found Him too much for Jesus' response to all this was,

No prophet is without honour except in his native place, among his own kindred, and in his own house. He could work no miracle there, apart from curing a few who were sick by lying hands on them, so much did their lack of faith distress him. He made the rounds of the neighbouring village instead, and spent his time teaching. (Mark 6:41–6)

Jesus then travelled to the region of Decapolis. It is written:

There some people brought to him a man who was deaf and could hardly talk, and they begged Jesus 'to place his hand on him'.

After he took him aside, away from the crowd, Jesus 'put his fingers into the man's ears'. Then he spit and 'touched the man's tongue'.

He looked up to heaven and with a deep sigh said to him, "Ephphatha!" (Which means "Be opened?").. At this, the man's ears were opened, his tongue was loosened and he began to speak plainly.

Jesus commanded them not to tell anyone. But the more he did so, the more they kept talking about it. People were overwhelmed with amazement. "He has done everything well," they said. He even makes the deaf hear and the mute speak. (Mark 7:31–37)

When they arrived at Bethsaida, some people brought him a blind man and begged him to touch him. Jesus took the blind man's hand and led him outside the village. Putting spittle on his eyes he laid his hands on him and asked, "Can you see anything?" The man opened his eyes and said, "I can see people but they look like walking trees!" Then a second time Jesus laid hands on his eyes, and he saw perfectly; his sight was restored and he could see everything clearly. Jesus sent him home with the admonition, "Do not even go into the village." (Mark 8:22–26)

The Gospel of Mark records that the Apostles had gone to drive out a malignant spirit from a young man, but they did not succeed. Then Jesus was called:

> *Jesus asked the boy's father, "How long has he been like this? From childhood, he answered. It has often thrown him into fire and water. You would think it would kill him. If out of kindness of your heart you can do anything to help us, please do! Jesus said. "Everything is possible for one who believes." Immediately the boy's father exclaimed, "I do believe; help me overcome my unbelief!" When Jesus saw that a crowd was running to the scene, he rebuked the impure spirit. "You deaf and mute spirit," he said, "I command you, come out of him and never enter him". The spirit shrieked, convulsed him violently and came out. The boy looked so much like a corpse that many said, "He's dead." But Jesus took him by the hand and lifted him to his feet, and he stood up. After Jesus had gone indoors, his disciples asked him privately, why couldn't we drive it out? He replied, "This kind can come out only by prayer." (Mark 9:21–29)*

The Ascension of Jesus

When Jesus rose from the dead, He appeared to the Apostles who were sitting at a table. He took them to task for their disbelief and their stubbornness since they had put no faith in those who had seen Him after He was raised from the dead.

He nevertheless empowered them all:

> *Then he told them: Go into the whole world and proclaim the good news to all creation. The man who believes in it and accepts baptism will be saved; the man who refuses to believe in it will be condemned. Signs like these will accompany those who have professed their faith: they will speak entirely new languages, they will be able to handle serpents, they will be able to drink poison without harm, and the sick upon whom they lay their hands will recover. (Mark 16:15–18)*

Hands in the Time of the Apostles

When Jesus finished his mission, he appeared to the Apostles:

> *Recall those words I spoke to you when I was still with you: everything written about me in the Law of Moses and the prophets and psalms had to be fulfilled."*
>
> *Then He opened their minds to the understanding of the Scriptures. "Thus it is written that the Messiah must suffer and rise from the dead on the third day. In his name penance for the remission of sins is to be preached to all the nations, beginning at Jerusalem. You are witnesses of this. See, I send down upon you the promise of my Father. Remain here in the city until you are clothed with power from on high."*
>
> *Then he led them out of Bethany, and 'with his hands upraised, blessed them'.*
>
> *As he blessed, he left them, and was taken up to heaven.*
>
> *They fell down to do him reverence, and then returned to Jerusalem filled with joy. There they were to be found in the temple constantly, speaking in praises of God. (Luke 24:50–53)*

Now begins the interesting development of the clothing with power from on High. Power in the hands of the Apostles, will it work?

The orans position in mosaic at the Roman catacomb

As the Apostles continued to fulfil Jesus' command of preaching to the world, they also continued to be harassed by the antagonistic High Priests of the Sanhedrin, The Apostles were brought in front of the Sanhedrin and scolded, but Peter replied that the power that raised Jesus from the dead came from God's own right hand: "By 'His own right hand God has now raised him' up to be leader and saviour, to give repentance and forgiveness of sins through him to Israel" (Acts 5:31).

As God's right hand guided them and gave them strength, the Apostles realized that the workload was too much for them. So they gathered the faithful and told them,

> It is not right for us to neglect the word of God in order to wait on tables. Look around among your number, brothers, for seven men acknowledged to be deeply spiritual and prudent, and we shall appoint them to this task. This will permit us to concentrate on prayer and the ministry of the word. "The proposal was unanimously accepted by the community.

> Following this they selected Stephen, a man filled with faith and the Holy Spirit; Philip, Prochorus, Nicanor, Timon, Parmenas, and Nicolaus of Antioch who had been a convert to Judaism. They presented these men to the apostles, who 'first prayed over them and then imposed hands on them'. (Act 6:2:7)

Just observe the result that the imposition of hands had on the expansion of the young church. The Word of God continued to spread while at the same time, the number of the disciples in Jerusalem increased enormously. We are told that over "four thousand men were baptized. There were many priests among those who embraced the faith". Another emphasis in this passage is the reference to "men"; since women were not mentioned simply because they did not figure importantly. In the Jewish tradition, or in the Census. But women, and children were surely also baptized.

It is in Luke's accounts that we start seeing women taking prominent roles in the mission of Jesus.

The above occasion was itself was a momentous one. The laying of hands in this instance was what we call the "transference of power, passing on authority" in the Apostolic tradition, from the Apostles to these seven deacons or Disciples. What we know today as Holy Orders, which the Apostolic Catholic Church has exercised through the centuries a vital requirement for exercising the functions of Priest and Bishops, the imposition of hands together with a prayer of consecration imparting the Holy Spirit.

Only the Greek Orthodox Church and other Easter Rite Churches, Syrian, Ethiopian Arminian, can claim this divine, unbroken transference of Apostolic Holy Orders, which gives validity in the carrying out of the apostolic/priestly functions. Today all the above-mentioned churches are invited to participate in the Synod of Bishops called from time to time by the Apostolic Catholic Church.

I have often thought that this is event is a clear biblical example of how, through the appointment of deacons, the Christian community grew. Would the modern church not grow significantly with a system of appointing deacons to aid the priests/pastors of the flock?

The story continues when the Apostle called Cephas, or Petrus—both names mean "Rock"—and John, the youngest of the Apostles and whom Jesus loved, were sent to Samaria. This was a significant mission since the Samaritans were the hated enemy of the Jews; they were a heretical Jewish sect.

The Samaritans were made famous by Jesus in two of His parables. One was the occasion when an individual was robbed and beaten on the road and left there. A couple of Jews passed him by on their way to the Temple in Jerusalem. One man, who we now call the Good Samaritan, stopped and helped him, and took him to an inn. He told the innkeeper to take care of him, and on his way back, he would take care of the man's expenses. Likewise, Jesus went to a well because He was thirsty and there met a Samaritan woman. He asked her for a drink of water. What Jesus did was an incredible thing. The astonished Samaritan woman asked him, "How come you a man and a Jew are asking me a woman and a Samaritan for a drink of water?" Even then He persisted and went on to tell her all about her life. Then he promised he would give her water that would give her eternal life! First she called him "Sir" then "Prophet" and then "Messiah". She went to her people and told them about this incredible man. Jesus spoke with them and stayed for two days, teaching the Samaritans there. Many more came to the faith (John 4:19:42).

Now the two Apostles, Peter and John, were on their way, hopefully, to complete the conversion of the Samaritan people. Some had become believers and followers of Christ and baptized in the manner of John's baptism by water. But they had not yet been baptized to receive the Holy Spirit. It is written:

> *The two went down to these people and prayed that they might receive the Holy Spirit. It had not yet come down upon them and they received the Holy Spirit. Simon, the magician, observed that it was through the laying on of hands that the apostles conferred the Spirit*

so much so that he offered money to Peter for the privilege of teaching him how to do this marvellous deed. Peter said in answer: "May you and your money rot—thinking that God's gift can be bought! You can have no portion or lot in this affair. Your heart is not steadfastly set on God. Reform you evil ways. Pray that the Lord may pardon you for thinking the way you have." (Acts 8:20)

Soon after, Saul a zealous Jew, who was persecuting Christians, was on his way to Damascus on horseback. He was stopped when a light flashed in his path. He fell off his horse to the ground and was blinded. Then he heard a voice speaking to him:

"Saul, Saul, why do you persecute me?" It is hard for you to kick goad." "I said at that, 'who are you sir?' "I am that Jesus who you are persecuting. Get up and stand on your feet. I have appeared to you to designate you as my servant and as a witness to what you have seen of me and what you will see of me. I have delivered you from this people and from the nations to open the eyes of those to whom I am sending you, to turn them from darkness to light and from the dominion of Satan to God; that through their faith in me they may obtain the forgiveness of their sins and portion among God's people. (Acts 26:14–18)

A disciple named Ananias was ordered by the Lord Jesus to go to Saul. Ananias went reluctantly since Saul was a known persecutor of the followers of Jesus. When Ananias entered the house and met Saul, he laid hands on Saul and said,

"Saul, my brother, I have been sent by the Lord Jesus who appeared to you on the way here, to help you recover your sight and filled with the Holy Spirit." Immediately something like scales fell from his eyes and he regained his sight. He got up and was baptized, and his strength returned to him after he had taken food. Saul stayed some time with the disciple in Damascus and soon began to proclaim in the synagogues that Jesus was the Son of God. Any who heard it were greatly taken aback. They kept saying, "Isn't this the man who worked such havoc in Jerusalem among those who invoke this name?" (Acts 9:4–19)

As the Faith was spreading and while the Church in Antioch (present-day Turkey) was engaged in the liturgy of the Lord and fasting, the Holy Spirit spoke to them: "Set apart Barnabas and Saul for me to do the work for which I have called them. Then, after they had fasted and prayed, they imposed hands on them and sent them off" (Acts 13:1–4).

Here is a demonstration of the power that exists when fasting is accompanied by prayer in the gathering of Christians. The commissioning of the disciples sent to evangelize to the ends of the world was a grandiose plan inspired by the Holy Spirit, who together with the Father and Son accompanied the disciples in their dangerous and far-reaching world mission that would have lasting effects when they preached to virtual pagans. The Jew Pharisee-trained Saul was now converting Gentiles, non-Jews, to Christianity.

The disciples travelled to the island of Cyprus. It is written:

> *They came across a Jewish magician named Bar-Jesus who posed as a prophet. He was close to the court of the pro-consular governor Segious Paulus, who had also summoned Barnabas and Saul and was anxious to hear the word of God. But Bar-Jesus opposed them and sought to turn the governor away from the faith. Saul known as Paul was filled with the Holy Spirit; he stared at him and exclaimed "you are an imposter and a thorough fraud, you son of Satan and enemy of all that is right! Will you never stop trying to make crooked the straight path of the Lord? The Lord's hand is upon you even now! For a time you shall be blind, unable so much as to see the sun." At once a misty darkness came over him, and he groped about for someone to lead him by the hand. When the governor saw what had happened, he believed, so impressed was he by the teaching about the Lord. (Acts 13:6–12)*

In this case, the hand of the Lord gave no benefit to Bar-Jesus.

When Paul arrived in Ephesus (present-day Greece), he met some disciples who had been baptized in the baptism of John for the repentance of sins, so Paul quickly baptized them in the name of Jesus. "As Paul laid his hands on them, the Holy Spirit came down on them and they began to speak in tongues and to utter prophecies. There were in the company about twelve men in all" (Acts 19:6).

This is but one example of the power given by the Holy Spirit to the disciples in the discharge of their evangelization that enabled the faith to spread throughout. In this last instance, we hear that the Holy Spirit gave these disciples two spiritual gifts called the gifts of the Holy Spirit. One was speaking in tongues, and the other was prophesying: "Meanwhile God worked extraordinary miracles at the hands of Paul" (Acts 19:5–11).

And so the Apostles dispersed in different directions, spreading the Good News to the poor that the kingdom of heaven was at hand. And with a renewed spiritual power, we hear in Paul's letter to Timothy exhorting him, "Until I arrive, devote yourself to reading of Scripture, to preaching and teaching. Do not neglect the gift you received when, as a result of prophecy the presbyters laid their hands on you" (1 Timothy 4:13–16).

The body of elders was no less the other Apostles who had formed this new church, which was spreading like wildfire.

Now back to Paul and his journey to Ephesus, he found some disciples and asked about their baptisms:

> *"Did you receive the Holy Spirit when you became believers?" "We have not so much heard that there is a Holy Spirit." "Well how were you baptized?" he persisted. They replied, "With the baptism of John."*

> *Paul then explained, "John's baptism was a baptism of repentance. He used to tell people about the one who would come after him in whom they were to believe—that is Jesus." When they heard this, they were baptized in the name of the Lord Jesus.*

> *As Paul placed his hands on them, the Holy Spirit came on them, and they spoke in tongues and prophesied. (Acts 19:2–7)*

Further in his letter, Paul warns Timothy, "Never lay hands hastily on anyone or you may be sharing in the misdeeds of others. Keep yourself pure" (1 Timothy 5:22).

In his second letter to Timothy, Paul reminds him with these words:

> *For this reason, I remind you to stir into flame the gift of God bestowed when my hands were laid on you. The Spirit God has given us is no cowardly spirit, but rather one that makes us strong, loving and wise. Therefore, never be ashamed of your testimony to our Lord, nor of*

me, a prisoner for his sake; but with the strength which comes from God bear our share of the hardship which the gospel entails. (2 Timothy 1:6–8)

In Paul's wonderful letter to the Hebrew, the exhortation to faithfulness is very clear, as is the power that is given by the Holy Spirit when it says:

In view of this, we must attend all the more to what we have heard, lest we drift away. For if the word spoken through angels stood unchanged, all transgression and disobedience received its due punishment, how shall we escape if we ignore a salvation as great as ours? Announced first by the Lord, it was confirmed to us by those who had heard him. God then gave witness to it by signs, miracles, varied acts of power, and distribution of the gift of the Holy Spirit as he willed. (Heb. 2:1–4)

The distribution of the gift of the Holy Spirit with various acts of power included the power that came through prayer and the "laying of hands, speaking in tongues and prophesying".

Teaching to a now maturing congregation, Paul writes to tell them, "Let us, then, go beyond the initial teaching about Christ and advance to maturity, not laying the foundation all over again: repentance from dead works, instruction about baptism and the laying on of hands, resurrection of the dead, and eternal judgement. And God permitting we shall advance!" (Heb. 6:1–3).

CHAPTER 5

The Altar Call of Love: The Eucharist

Why the title, "The Altar Call of Love"? I call the Eucharist an altar call of love. No one can deny that all the things Jesus Christ said and did; He said and did them with perfect love.

At the Eucharist God calls us to come forward and receive Him bodily. His act of love is consummated with our participation.

The Eucharist

The message of love as a guiding principle and way of life is one of the many things that sets Christianity apart from all other religions because, "God is Love" (John 4:8). *Agape!* The love of God is the only powerful means by which our society can be changed. This power lies within the Christian Church, whose mission it is to evangelize to spread the Good News of salvation and love.

The Father's greatest gift to us was His incarnate Son, Jesus Christ. That He chose to become man, suffer, and die for our sins is the most beautiful and greatest of mysteries. It was His intended plan of salvation and for the redemption of humankind's sins.

Jesus said,

> The Father loves me for this: that I lay down my life to take it up again. (John 10:17)

> There is no greater love than this: to lay down one's life for one's friend. (John 15:13)

We need to follow the biblical Jewish tradition of sacrifice to understand what redemption and sacrifice entails in the context of Jesus' crucifixion.

The Jewish paschal meal and Jesus' crucifixion sacrifice are intrinsically bound together. The paschal celebration of the Passover reminds Jews all over the world not to forget their escape from bondage and liberation from slavery.

In His paschal meal, Jesus intended that we not forget our own liberation/redemption and His sacrifice for us. He also wants us to remember Him by following what He commanded us to do: "You will live in my love if you keep my commandments" (John 15:10).

Jesus did this out of the purest of love. It is His gift to us with the promise of eternal life. It came from the source of all love, "For God is Love", and, "we love because he loved us first" (1 John 4:8, 19). We share in His love, as Paul says, "Is not the cup of blessing we bless a sharing in the blood of Christ? And is not the bread we break a sharing in the body of Christ?"

The practise of celebrating the paschal meal He now transposes as the Eucharist, or "thanksgiving". Thanksgiving for what? For the great sacrifice of redemption and forgiveness of sins for all.

The direct command Jesus makes, which He intends us to keep, is, "This is my body to be given up for you. Do this as a remembrance of me" (Luke 22: 19).

Fifty years ago, I endeavoured to find some written explanation on the Eucharist. This had to be an explanation that provided scriptural references, explained the Judo-Christian tradition of the paschal meal, and related, in no uncertain way the earliest tradition of the Church and its understanding of the Eucharist as Paul asserted above.

So what is an altar call? "Altar call" is a term used in evangelical, Pentecostal, and charismatic circles that can mean God calling you personally to Him, as in the case of Abraham, Moses, Isaiah, the Apostles, or you coming to Him through a spiritual calling in a church gathering. It also means just walking up to Him at the altar with a heart full of spiritual desire and trusting Him with all your mind, heart, and soul. Coming down the aisle to the Altar to partake of the bread and wine is our response to the call of God's love. In the Eucharist, we actually walk down the aisle to the altar to receive Him bodily. We come forward for forgiveness and grace.

During my visit to Trinidad and Tobago, when I met Bishop McKinney, I had the opportunity to mention that I was writing about the altar call of love. He replies, "What a novel idea because when we come to the Eucharist, we forget that we are coming forward to a banquet and don't realize what is on the table." To my great joy, during his sermon during a mass he celebrated in Trinidad he went on to use the theme of the altar of love and the great banquet in front of us.

I had never questioned or doubted my church's teaching on the mystery of the body and blood of Jesus Christ present in the Eucharist. I always believed in it explicitly, but I still needed to learn more about it.

We now explore the tradition and scriptural meaning of the Eucharist.

In his letter addressed to all the bishops of the church, Pope John Paul II (now St John Paul II) he explains, among other things, something I find very refreshing, particularly for the future of such a festive occasions as the celebration of the Eucharist, the thanksgiving. He said, "We shall continue in the future to take special care to promote and follow the renewal of the Church according to the teachings of The Second Vatican Council, in the spirit of an ever living tradition." Here we have the seed of wisdom—always renewal, always vigilant, always guiding, and always faithful to the apostolic heritage.

The problem of the real presence of Christ in the Eucharist came under attack during the Reformation of the sixteenth century and the start of various forms of Protestantism. However, to counter the many erroneous ideas that this challenge brought, the Catholic Church held its own Ecumenical Council of Trent, which affirmed and entrenched the ancient apostolic views on the Eucharist and many other matters.

The Council taught the principle of Eucharistic concomitance, that "Christ whole and entire, and a true Sacrament are received under either species," so the faithful need not receive from the chalice.

The twenty-second session set down the true doctrine concerning the Holy sacrifice of the Mass against the novelties of the Protestants. This states that, "the Sacrifice of the Mass is propitiatory both for the living and the dead."

J. P. Kirsch succinctly summarizes the importance of the Council of Trent:

> The Ecumenical Council of Trent has proved to be of the greatest importance for the development of the inner life of the Church. No council has ever had to accomplish its task under more serious difficulties; none has had so many questions of the greatest importance to decide. The assembly proved to the world that notwithstanding repeated apostasy in church life there still existed in it in abundance of religious force and of loyal championship of the unchanging principles of Christianity".

> It is true that the Catholic Church, in the Council of Trent 'Entrenched' itself and threw its arms around the priceless list of faith and covered with its arms, for protection, to guard the basic credos of faith that had been fought over in the early centuries. The theological struggle that took place over the Credo was monumental, as it had been in the beginning.

As Jesus started to become real in my life, as I received the Eucharist, this occasion has often brought me joyful tears.

For the first time I understood what the "Penitent Woman" (Mary Magdalene?) must have experienced at the feet of Jesus when she wept, and her tears fell upon His feet. She anointed His feet with perfumed oils, wiped His feet dry with her hair. These were tears of purification and joy that come through with the nearness of Jesus' anointing the glow of His glory, His love and compassion embracing her. At that moment, the sinful woman Mary was experiencing her conversion for we are told "seven devils" had been cast out of her. The seven devils were the seven cardinal sins of lust, covetousness, greed, sloth, pride, anger, and hate. What this woman experienced was the joyful peace of His presence at the time of her conversion. These tears of hers were a gift.

The well-known Jesuit Francis Sullivan, SJ, wrote:

> When does weeping qualify as the Gift of tears? It seems to me that when it both signifies and intensifies such an attitude as contrition for sin compassion with the suffering Christ, or Joy in the experience of consolation. In other words to experience conversion is to experience His mercy, His anointing, that, is a happy occasion!

If I believe that the God's Word was the source of life, and this life brought light to humankind (John 1:4–5), then when God speaks, do things happen?

Does He mean what He says? I believe that when Jesus said, "I am the Way, the Truth and the Life" (John 14:6), "I am the Light of the world" (John 8:12), "I am the Bread of Life" (John 6:35), and, "and He would give you life-giving water" (John 4:10), Jesus meant what He said!

God's power is limitless, awesome, inexplicable, and incomprehensible by our human standards and knowledge. If as a believer I question what Jesus says, I question God's very existence. So when Jesus says to His Disciples, "I have food to eat that you know nothing about" (John 4:32), am I going to suppose that I know better? But we may ask, what is the food that we know nothing of?

In John 1:14, the entrance of the Word into the world was spoken of in terms of becoming "flesh", a human being. But now it is "living Bread," in the form of Jesus, but now in the form of bread and wine.

> Who am I to question Jesus when He emphatically says, "This is my Body", or, "this is my Blood"? When He says, "This is," I take it to mean *This is*! It does not mean, this could be, this is like, this represents, this symbolizes, or this is similar to. No! The metaphoric understanding of His listeners had already been changed to the real understanding of these words. Emphatically, *"This is!"*

It is important at this point for us to re-read John 6:25–71.

How can this man give us His flesh to eat (John 6:52)? Good question.

Everyone understood the spiritual language that Jesus was using when He said about Himself, "I am the Light, the Truth, and the Way." Yet it is quite possible that at the time, they did not fully appreciate that Jesus really meant what He was saying about being all these things. But what He said about being the, "bread that came down from heaven", and about, "eat my flesh, drink my blood", together with the increased emphasis that Jesus gave to the word "eat" (trógó) created an uproar in His listeners unprecedented in the whole of the Jewish tradition. Even his own Disciples, all Jews, reacted adversely to these references. They had never heard Him make such strong statements, and this kind of language was new to them (Raymond Brown SJ on John chapter 6:34–64).

Several times Jesus got a negative and reactionary response from the crowd following Him. True, Jesus had spoken before to Pharisees and Scribes, but they had closed minds. However, those listening who followed Him were a different crowd. This crowd had seen the incredible miracles He performed, in particular the multiplication of the loaves and fishes, and multiple healings; they now hung on to every word He spoke. There were no pagans in that crowd. These were Jews, and His words did not go down well!

Yet instead of correcting Himself and saying to this vast crowd, "Don't go. I only meant this or that. I was only speaking metaphorically", and so on, Jesus went on. And according to John, who would have defended Jesus' meaning with his very life, especially since he was writing this gospel several decades after the event, takes great care to dispel the notion that Jesus is simply referring to ordinary bread. John makes Jesus out to be insistent, pedantic, and uncompromising when explaining the difference between the manna from heaven sent to the Jewish people in the desert and the bread He gave to the multitude and His "flesh and blood".

As we read the Gospel of John, it also becomes clear that when John writes and makes people misunderstand, he does this as a means to give Jesus an opportunity to explain more deeply. In many statements that Jesus makes he usually starts by saying, "I firmly assure you." Though in this instance, when the people grumbled during this particular discourse, He makes this holy affirmation. He does not explain away what He said. Instead, He goes on to solemnly reinforce what He said.

How beautifully He reminds them of the multiplication of the loaves, the manna in the desert, and then skilfully guides His audience to another topic, preparing them for the gift of all gifts. He affirms: "I am telling you the truth, you are looking for me because you ate the bread and had all you wanted" (John 6:26).

What Moses gave you was not the bread from heaven. (John 6:32)

Your ancestors ate manna in the desert, but they died. (John 6:49)

For the bread that God gives is He who comes down from heaven and gives life to the world. (John 6:33)

I am the bread of Life. (John 6:35)

I am the bread that came down from Heaven. (John 6:41)

On hearing these, the crowd simply grumbled, but Jesus does not explain. Instead He insisted, "The bread that I will give him is my flesh" (John 6:51). Now this appears to be too much for them for they could not accept this, and what ensued was pandemonium. At this time the Jews quarrelled among themselves, saying, "How can he give us his flesh to eat?" (John 22:52).

Curiously, Jesus has another opportunity to clarify the obvious confusion, but He does not. He continues, "If anyone eats this bread, he will live forever. The bread that I will give is my flesh, which I give so that the world may live" (John 22:58). Ask yourself this: Why would John write like this? Why would Jesus rub it in, upset them, and make them uncomfortable if he did not mean what he said?

This was not a parable Jesus was telling them. These people could be forgiven for not understanding what He was telling them. They were His followers. They had walked for miles and crossed the lake, and they wanted to believe. After all, Jesus, as a Jew, who faithfully followed the Law, knew how touchy His Jewish followers were about these things. But instead, the man who had said, "I have come to fulfil the Law not to do away with the Law", was now saying, "Let me solemnly assure you, if you do not eat the flesh of the Son of Man and drink His blood, you have no life in you. He who feeds on my flesh and drinks my blood has life eternal" (John 6:53–58). What a stand He took! What a confrontation!

Drinking blood was against Jewish Law. This Law was not done away with by Jesus because the prohibition of drinking blood was also imposed on the early Christians (Acts 15:20). In fact, Gentiles were being instructed to follow the Jewish Law of not drinking blood. Yet on the other hand, circumcision, a strict requirement under the Jewish covenant, was not a requirement for being a believer in Christ.

Jesus is seen here making an exception to the Law. His blood was to be drunk! This is what the Jewish crowd was hearing. This was an anathema.

The crowd understood Him so clearly because of His choice of words that we are told, "Many of his followers heard this and said, 'this teaching is too hard. Who can listen to it?' … because of this many of Jesus' followers turned back and would not go with Him any more" (John 6:60).

What Jesus was saying to them was repulsive, violent, and unacceptable. But for whom? Too many of His followers. Not bystanders, critics, or rivals but His followers. Why would His followers want to leave Him? One would have thought that after seeing Him working so many wonders and signs, speaking with so much authority, getting the best of the Pharisees and Sadducees, they would wish to continue to follow Him and believe anything He did or said. Yet they rejected him.

This sounded very much like cannibalism, paganism. Jesus had departed from Jewish religious tradition. Ironically enough, during the persecution of the early Christians, one of the accusations levelled at them was that they practised cannibalism.

This rejection by Jews persisted into the third century. Origin of Alexandrian (200–253), in answer to Celsus's allegations against Christianity, alludes to Jewish charges that Christians ate human flesh.

Celsus was a pagan anti-Christian philosopher who attempted to bring into disrepute what are termed the "Love Feasts" of the Christians he claimed were in violation of Roman law. He also wrote that Judaism, upon which Christianity depended, was barbaric in its origin.

Kilmartin, in his *Chalice Dispute*, suggests that the consistent emphasis on drinking the blood is directed against Jewish-Christian Gnostic circles, who opposed the use of the chalice in the Eucharist service because of their deep-rooted aversion to blood.

However, if John was not sensitive to Jewish sensibilities and goes on insisting on the reality of the flesh and blood of Christ, he does not go to the other extreme of attributing magical powers to the reception of the flesh and blood of Jesus, which would compare this Christian sacrament with a pagan mystery. Instead, what John does is to teach about obtaining eternal life through believing in the reception of the flesh and blood (John. 6:41–54), not just believing in Jesus alone, but believing in what they were eating.

So here we find ourselves back to the same questions. Why would Jesus insist on such a repulsive action from His followers? Why would He allow—nay, force—so many followers to leave him? Was this not the same Jesus who gave us the parable of the lost sheep? He was the Good Shepherd and would not allow one single sheep to get lost!

Earlier He had assured them, "I will never turn away anyone who comes to me … it is the will of Him who sent me that I should not lose any of those He has given me" (John 6:37). Yet here He was, driving away not just one sheep but nearly the whole flock!

John was the gospel writer who stated that Jesus always knew what His listeners were thinking. Knowing what they were thinking, would He not have used a more acceptable Jewish explanation? Why would He encourage the grumbling which was in fact cries of rejection, angry arguments, dissention, and eventually, knowingly allow many of His followers to desert Him? He was driving them away from the prospect of eternal life. And by driving them away With His provocative choice of words, He was casting them into eternal darkness! Are we to believe that all of this was because He did not make Himself clear? It does not make any sense whatsoever that Jesus would have purposely been ambiguous on the very reason for His incarnation, His message of salvation.

This crowd of followers had come to Him because the word had already gone out that He was the Messiah. Are we to accept that the Saviour Himself unwittingly lost these followers?

So strong was the negative reaction from the Disciples that Jesus had to ask His trusted followers, "Do you want to leave me too?" It looks like at that moment everyone had left, and the only ones remaining were His very hesitant but faithful hand-picked friends. Simon Peter answered Him, "Lord, to whom shall we go? … and now we believe and know that you are the Holy One who has come from God."

They did not yet understand for they had not yet received the Holy Spirit, but they believed what He was telling them this was truly faith in action! They believed what everyone else failed to understand—that Jesus was God and was talking to them as God, and His powerful Word made everything possible.

Because of our limited understanding, He used human and words to reveal His true nature. Christ was teaching Christ, and Christ was teaching about God.

Some might still disagree over the interpretation of this teaching of Jesus. I see this present-day understanding and reaction to this teaching no different from that of the original crowd to whom Jesus spoke. But apart from the evidence of the reaction of the crowd, John the Evangelist, inspired by the Holy Spirit in writing this account, chose certain words deliberately to drive his point home. John could have quoted Jesus as having used many other words when it came to this passage about, "eating his flesh". Raymond Brown, a noted Catholic biblical scholar, in his commentary on the Gospel of John says that all the following Greek words have been used in the inspired Gospels and letters:

> Estho: To eat (as distinct from pino, to drink) (Heb. 10:27); metaphorically to "devour".
> Of ordinary food and drink (1 Cor. 9–7; 11–22)
> Of partaking food at table (Mark 2:16)
> Of revelling (Matt. 24:49; Luke 12:45)
> Phago: To eat, devour, consume (Luke 8:55); used eleven times in 1 Corinthians.
> Bibroski: To eat eagerly (John 6:13).
> Kataphagh: To eat up (John 2:17; Rev. 9:10).
> Korahnnumi: To satiate, to satisfy with food (Acts 27:38; 1 Cor. 4:8).

But John, in trying to illustrate why Jesus' followers left Him, starts in fact to use his literary skills and emphasizes the Lord's use of different Greek words which under normal circumstances, mean virtually the same thing. But he changes the action words "esthio" and "phago") to a stronger word "trógó." This is very noticeable. John is stressing to his readers to be under no illusions as to what Jesus meant! The more emphasis he placed on the word "eat", the more persistent the unbelief of His hearers!

In verses 49 to 53 the word "phago" is used, but in verses 54 and 58, the word "trógó" is used. And in verse 58, trógó is put into immediate contrast with phago. The use of "trógó" in John 13:18 is witness to eating real food. However, trógó signifies more than just eating. It signifies to gnaw, chew, and bite. It stresses the deliberate and slow process of consuming.

We can now appreciate exactly why the crowd understood what Jesus was asking them to do and how impossible it was for them to follow Him.

The Passover Meal became the Last Supper

As in the account of the storm at sea (4:35), Jesus is also called "Teacher", and a teaching is about to take place! That teaching will come in the form of a deed or action. Jesus' action is a teaching that would guide and sustain His followers.

In the Last Supper we have a teaching or lesson, something the Apostles had to listen to and take note of. At a meal like the Seder, the ceremonial food is explained; each item has a special meaning in the history of the Jewish people. Jesus and His disciples were celebrating what amounted to the Passover meal, a meal with a ritual that had been celebrated annually by Jews all over the world since the time of the great Exodus.

Normally, 2 verses from Deuteronomy 26:58 are read:

> And thou shall speak and say before the Lord thy God: "A wandering Aramean was my parent, and they went down into Egypt, and sojourned there, few in number; and became there a nation, great, mighty, and populous. And the Egyptians dealt ill with us, and afflicted us, and laid upon us hard bondage. And we cried unto the Lord, the God of our parents, and the Lord heard our voice, and saw our affliction, and our toil, and our oppression. And the Lord brought us forth out of Egypt with a strong hand and an outstretched arm, and with great terribleness, and with signs, and with wonders."

Then the ten plagues that befell the Egyptians are retold. Psalms are sung. Hands are washed. The blessings over the matzahs and bitter herbs are said. There is Grace after the meal with a first recital of Birkat Hamazan. Hallels (songs of praise) are sung, Psalms 113 and 114, and then Psalms 115 to 118, as well as Psalm 136. Of course the ritual may vary depending on local tradition.

After this the fourth cup of wine is drunk and a brief grace for the "fruit of the vine" is said.

We are not told if Jesus does the same thing.

Jesus and friends settled in to what the Disciples thought was going to be a normal and familiar celebration. Prayers; songs; praise; a little teaching; the blessing of bread, wine, and bitter herbs; and possibly marinated fish. The Jewish wine was so rich and pure that a drop of water would be added to the wine at the time of the blessing, to symbolically dilute the wine, not in strength, but in its purity because to Jews, only God was totally pure. They did not count on the turn of event. Jesus did give them a lesson, but it was not little! Instead of saying the usual blessing handed down to Jews over the centuries, Jesus changed the traditional blessing. What we are told is that He "invests" the bread and wine with new meaning that bread and wine had never had before.

He took a piece of bread (as expected), said a prayer of thanks (as expected), broke it, and gave it out (as expected). But then He said, "Take and eat it (trogo) this is my body" (not expected).

Similarly, He took the wine and said, "This is my blood the blood covenant, to be poured out in behalf of many for the forgiveness of sins" (Matt. 26:28).

His Disciples must have remembered vividly His discourse on the bread of life, when He said to the crowd, "'I am the bread of life', warning them, 'Let me solemnly assure you, if you do not eat (Trogo)the flesh of the Son of Man and drink his blood you have no life in you'" (John 6:53).

At that moment we detect an air of peace and tranquillity, even acceptance of the moment. There was no opposition to Jesus' statement. They probably still did not realize how special an occasion this was for John, who sat next to Jesus at the table, tells us, "There was, of course, no Spirit as yet, since Jesus had not yet been glorified" (John 1:39).

But the Spirit would come to them after Jesus' ascension. Jesus's Disciples might not have understood, but there was expectancy in the air since He said,

> "It is much better for you that I go. If I fail to go, the Paraclete will never come to you, whereas if go, I will send him to you … When he comes, however, being the Spirit of

Truth he will guide you to all truth … As the Father has sent me so I send you. Receive the Holy Spirit." (John 16:1, 13; 20:21–22)

After He died and rose from the dead, and when the feast of Pentecost came and found all the Disciples gathered in the upper room, the Holy Spirit, as promised by Jesus, came upon the Apostles and Mary, His mother. The truth that Jesus spoke about was finally revealed to them. The significance of the "breaking of the bread" and His discourse on the "Bread of Life" was finally clear to them. The Paraclete, the Helper, the Advocate would teach and make them remember all (John 14:26).

In the course of this new revelation, they probably also realized the deeper meaning of what Jesus meant when He said, "I have wanted so much to eat 'this Passover' meal with you before I suffer" (Luke 22:15), as well as when He said, "For I tell you, I will not eat again until it is given its full meaning in the kingdom of God" (Luke 22:15–16).

"This Passover?" What Passover?

Was it just the meal He was looking forward to, or could it possibly be His own Passover? For Jesus had chosen a special occasion to explain a soul-shaking new way of remaining always with his followers. He said, "Until it is given its full meaning in the kingdom of God!" Wait a minute. What had John the Baptist said when he saw Jesus approaching? "Look there is the Lamb of God!" (John 1:36). Of course that was it. Jesus had taken the place of the Passover lamb.

The lamb that John mentions in Revelation, which appeared with the wounds of suffering, was "The lamb that had been slain" (Rev. 5:6), though victorious! It was now clear that Jesus had offered Himself in sacrifice in the same way the Jews had been commanded by God to sacrifice and eat the lamb before the big escape, the escape from slavery and the journey to the Promised Land (Exod. 12:21–28).

Jesus, the new Passover lamb, was offering them His flesh to nourish and build up the chosen people into the people of God on their way to the New Jerusalem, the Kingdom of God.

What excitement they must have felt at the revelation and understanding they received with the outpouring of the Holy Spirit. As Jews they regarded every death of an innocent person as an atoning death, and they now saw Jesus' death in this light. They were aware of several scriptural connections with this idea of sacrifice (Exod. 24:8–11) and of the New Covenant (Jer. 31:34), as well as with the idea of the atoning sufferings of the servant of God (Isa. 53:12).

The evangelists, it seems to me, who was writing long after the event, was able to mesh all these revelations together in their composition of the Gospels prompted by the Holy Spirit. They now understood that by distributing the bread and wine and invoking the blessing, "Take this, this is my body and blood" (Mark 14:22–24) in the names of the Father, the Son, and the Holy Spirit, Jesus had indicated to them that they were to share in His sacrifice continuously and in the power of His atoning death: "Do this as a remembrance of me" (Luke 22:19).

Greek Meaning of the Word "Eat"

The word "eat" in Greek has various and confusing meanings. An interesting observation has been made here by scripture scholar Raymond Brown, SJ, on John's chapter 6, specifically verses 24 through 54.

The use of the word "body" in the three synoptic Gospels and Paul is used as "soma" and "body", which is an appropriate Greek translation. But in Hebrew and Aramaic, the language used by Jesus, there was no word for body. The word "guph" was later used for body but only when referring to it as a corpse. The normal Semitic formula for referring to the human components were "flesh and blood".

So the Apostles and the Christian communities which followed them saw their fellowship meals in a new light. Jesus had commanded them to "Do this as a remembrance of me. This cup is the new covenant in my blood which shall be shed for you." (Luke 22: 17-20).

This command implied total acceptance of His actions. He intended them to relive the memory of His sacrifice. Together with His promise that He would be present among those who gathered in His name (Matt. 18:20).

Christians believe that in the celebration of the Eucharist, the body and blood of Jesus are actually made present. The moment in which Jesus becomes present is known as the Anamnesis. This sacramental change occurs at all times and in all places where the Eucharist is celebrated. It happens when the priest blesses the bread and wine and says, "This is". The blessing does not merely recall, it relives that moment when Jesus blessed the bread and the wine at the Last Supper.

They had come to understand that God had given them two kinds of bread. This became their faith (John 6:32–56). The first bread was the Word that we hunger for. Scripture becomes our bread with the vital life of Christ in it.

The other bread is Christ Himself: "My flesh is real food," and, "my blood is real drink (John 6:55–56).

The humanity of Christ partaken of at the Eucharist is His body and blood ascended into the realm of God, filled and transformed by the Holy Spirit, the Anamnesis. The Eucharistic presence of the Lord is not limited to His earthly presence of His state but also to the realm of the Holy Spirit. "It is the Spirit that gives life; the flesh is useless" (John 6:63). This was John's way of explaining to his young Christian community the mystery of the real presence of Christ in the Eucharist.

Of the main things that Jesus commanded His followers to do, baptism and the Eucharist are the two specific signs or rituals which Jesus Himself instituted for us to do as a condition of our salvation so as to enjoy everlasting life.

As we go along we shall see how impressive this Eucharistic (thanksgiving) celebration must have been to Jesus' Disciples.

On the Road to Emmaus

Scripture says that after the resurrection, two of Jesus' followers unexpectedly met a traveller they didn't know on the road to Emmaus (Luke 24:13). Since it was late, they invited the stranger to eat with them.

We are then told that they stopped to eat. Jesus took the bread (as expected), probably because He was the senior of the three, said the blessing, broke it, and gave it to them. As expected? No, this was not as expected because—wait for this—"When He had seated Himself with them to eat, He took bread, pronounced the blessing, then broke the bread and began to distribute it to them. With that their eyes were opened and they recognised Him!" (Luke 24:30–31). Unknowingly they had invited Jesus to eat with them. So what opened their eyes? Jesus had walked with and spoken to them, explaining the scriptures. And later they said they had felt, "their hearts burning within them", and yet they did not recognize Him. But now, with the breaking of bread and with the unique words of the blessing—it must have been a unique blessing—they must have remembered His words: "This is my body given for you; do this in remembrance of me." Now the penny dropped!

The emphasis was not so much on meeting Jesus Himself that the Gospel writer is stressing here, but the breaking of bread. How else could this action be so special for three Jewish men since No stranger was refused water or bread on the road; travellers always shared everyone else's food. The eating of the bread was revealing, even if the bread was theirs in the first place.

Following His sudden departure, the two came alive and excitedly rushed to find the other Disciples and tell them of their meeting with the resurrected Christ and how it came about. They knew for sure, without a doubt, that it was truly Him in the breaking of bread.

Jewish Tradition, Christian Practise

We must not forget that it was Yahweh Himself who encouraged animal sacrifices as we read about in chapter 2. However, Paul writes, "… so God does away with all the old sacrifices and puts the sacrifice of Christ in their place" (Heb. 10:8–9). It is true that there is no further need for sacrifices of animals because Christ's sacrifice was done once and for all.

But look what Paul was doing in the Temple: "I had come to bring alms to my own people (the Jews) and to make my offerings. That is what I was doing when they found me in the temple court completing the rites of purification" (Acts 24:17). Paul had gone to the Temple to make his offerings. What was this offering? When Mary and Joseph went to the Temple to dedicate Jesus to the service of the Lord, they brought an offering, a pair of turtle doves.

Here Paul was observing the Jewish tradition of making an offering, but he was not sacrificing an animal. Jesus came, "not to do away with the Law, but to fulfil it", since he observed all the Jewish laws and traditions. During His lifetime, Jesus observed all the holy Jewish feasts, including the Feast of Atonement, which was rich in rituals and sacrifices. However, as for the Last Supper, according to Paul, "God does away with all the old sacrifices."

Jewish Converts

In the Acts of the Apostles, we read that thousands of Jews believed and followed Christ, yet the Jewish authorities refused to accept change. But it is not correct to say that the Jews did not believe in Jesus until Paul came into the scene. The Apostles, soon after the resurrection, evangelized principally among the Jews in Israel in Jesus' time. Even Paul is found preaching in the synagogues to the Jews of the Diaspora, Syria, Turkey, Greece, and Rome. That is why we find the Gospel writers heavily criticizing the Pharisees, Scribes, and Sadducees. It is only necessary to read Peter's and Paul's discourses in Acts 2:14–42 and Acts 13:16–52 to get an idea of their effective preaching to the Jewish people and the conversion which followed.

In the sixth chapter of Acts, Luke recounts how the pro-Christ community in Jerusalem was spreading fast, and how the Apostles, hard-pressed with pastoral care, found it necessary to add to their numbers by commissioning seven assistants, among them Stephen, Christianity's first martyr. Luke wrote, "So the word of God spread. The number of disciples in Jerusalem increased rapidly, the disciples in Jerusalem increased enormously. There were many priests among those who embraced the faith" (Acts 6:7).

It would be interesting to know how these Jewish priests—who had become followers of Jesus, accepting Him as the Messiah, all learned men of scripture and the Jewish Law, now following the new Judo-Christian way—influenced their concept of the Altar of sacrifice. And did they help to perpetuate what Jesus had done at the Last Supper? Were they the ones who realized the significance of the act of redemption that Jesus fulfilled?

These priests had embraced the fact that the Messiah had come to them, that they were harvesting the messianic promises of the prophets of old, particularly Isaiah, and that the Law was being fulfilled. They and the Apostles had followed implicitly and with fervour the Jewish faith with all its ramifications. Yet they accepted, too, all the new precepts that Jesus introduced. We could say that the party of the Nazarene, followers of the "New Way" were the first New Testament "Jews for Jesus". (Acts 24:5–14)

Again Paul, who had been accused by the Jews of blaspheming, tells the governor of Caesarea, "I admit to you that it is according to the new way -which they (the Jews) call a sect- that I worship the God of our Fathers. At the same time, I believe all that is written in the law and the prophets" (Act 24:14).

On the whole, we can say that it is not correct to assert that the Jews did not accept and believe that Jesus was the Messiah. The New Testament writings, except for Luke, were written by Jews, mostly for Jews, about a Jew.

But we can ask ourselves, where is the break with the Jewish tradition? When a man asked Jesus how he could he be saved, Jesus answered,

> Another time a man came up to him and said, "Teacher, what good must I do to possess everlasting life?" He answered, "Why do you question me about what is good? I you wish to enter into life, keep the commandments." Which ones?" He asked. Jesus replied, "You shall not kill; you shall not commit adultery; you shall not steal; you shall not bear false witness; Honour your father and your mother; and Love your neighbour as yourself;"

> The young man said to him, "I have kept all these, what do I need to do further?" Jesus told him, "If you seek perfection, go sell your possessions and give it to the poor. You will then have treasure in heaven. Afterwards, come back and follow me." (Matt.19:21)

Is the issue in this exchange that it is possible to attain entry into heaven by keeping the Ten Commandments as prescribed under Jewish Law?

Separate and modified forms of worship yes, in the light of Jesus' new commandments, but a deliberate break with the core of Jewish tradition is not possible since the messianic value of Jesus' life and teachings is only valid if it continues and fulfils the messianic plan. Jesus Himself said, "I have not come to abolish the Law and the prophets. I have come not to abolish them, but to fulfil them."

We find support for this as we read Acts, James, and many of Paul's letters. Paul tells the followers, former pagans, to shun idols. He explains to them the difference between the Eucharist and pagan sacrifices.

We cannot but be impressed with Paul's first letter to the Corinthians. This is what we would call a corrective pastoral. Paul was scandalized and annoyed with the reports that had come to him about the way the Corinthian church was slipping, and how they had lost the significance and meaning of the "fellowship meals". He reminds them sternly of the sanctity, holiness, and worthiness of these meals, especially when it came to the breaking of the bread and drinking of the wine.

He also reminds them of the necessity to prepare themselves for these special occasions. Paul's tone and choice of words show that these gatherings had to be taken solemnly. The demands he makes of them are almost parallel to the preparations for purification that Jews knew were necessary prior to entering the Holy of Holies, to encounter the Lord of Lords in the sanctity of the Temple (1 Cor. 11:28).

Paul did not stress body cleanliness but rather a thorough examination of their lives, of repentance and of spiritual purification. Then, and only then could they eat of the bread and drink of the wine. By which we gather that this was no ordinary bread and wine. In fact, he goes on to say what these are by referring to the relevant verses. Paul calls his Corinthian flock explicitly to order and rebukes them. He tells them they will be judged for behaving sacrilegiously partaking, "for eating the bread unworthily and profaning and sinning against the body and blood of the Lord" (1 Cor. 11:27).

At this point it is worthwhile reading this chapter of Paul's. Paul starts this reprimand and clarification with, "For I received from the Lord what I passed onto you" (1 Cor. 11:23). Are we hearing correctly? Is he saying that the Lord gave this to him personally? Hold on, how can this be possible if Paul was not present at the Last Supper? He tells us he did not get this from the other Apostles or Disciples but from Jesus Himself!

It appears He took the trouble to inform Paul personally about what He instituted at the Last Supper.

Paul, no doubt under the instructions from Jesus, told the faithful, "For I received from the Lord the teaching that I pass on to you, that the Lord Jesus on the night he was betrayed, took a piece of bread; gave thanks to God, broke it, and said "This is my body which is given up for you. Do this in remembrance of me … This cup is the covenant in my blood. Do this, whenever you drink it, in remembrance of me" (1 Cor. 11:23–25).

Now Paul gives his explanation of his own understanding about this instruction which the Lord passed on to Paul and Paul passed on to his communities.

In Samuel 21:5 we read that when David was running away from Saul's attempt to kill him, he came across the priest of Nob and asked for bread for his men. The priest replied, "I have no ordinary bread on hand, only holy bread; if the men have abstained from women, you may eat that." It was recognized that a person had to be clean of defilement before eating holy bread.

Paul knew what Jesus had directed them to do: "If you bring your gift to the Altar and then recall that your brother has anything against you, leave your gift at the Altar go first to be reconciled with your brother, and then come and offer your gift" (Matt. 5:23–24). "Come to the table," Paul is saying, "well prepared and worthily meet your God."

Paul recognized a big difference between the holy bread from the priest of Nob, and bread made sacred by Jesus, who called this bread, "His body".

No doubt Paul would have reminded them of another occasion: "I am telling you the truth whoever believes in me will do what I do and greater far than these. Why? Because I go to the Father, and whatever you ask in my name I will do" (John 14:23, 12–13). And so we believe and do as He did in celebrating the Lord's Supper.

Communion "with Christ" and "in Christ" not only looks to the past event but also looks to the future, "until He comes again!" (1 Cor. 11:26).

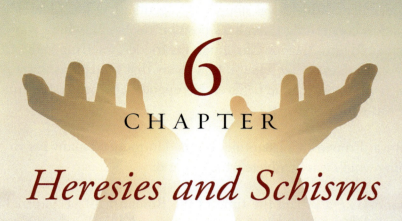

6
CHAPTER

Heresies and Schisms

Most information concerning heresies comes from the *Catholic Encyclopaedia*, the *Catholic History Dictionary, Dictionary of the Bible* (John L. McKenzie, SJ; *The Jerome Biblical Commentary* (Raymond E. Brown, SS, Joseph A. Fitzfmyer, SJ, Roland E. Murphy, O. Carm, Censores Deputati.

What Is Heresy?

In the following accounts I am attempting to give the reader an idea of the immense difficulties that faced faithful Christians, not only during the early centuries but even in the present time.

The faith flourished, and with it, many well-meaning but zealous church leaders flowered like mushrooms. And like mushrooms they spewed out spawn and propagated, each giving their own interpretations to the Gospels as known in those first, second, third, and fourth centuries of early Christianity, before the Gospels were compiled by St Jerome.

Human nature, being what it is, produced many well-meaning self-taught teachers across the Roman Empire, the then-known world. In their zealousness they introduced erroneous teachings about Christ and His message.

We are wrong if we think that this only happened in those long-gone centuries. It is happening today.

The other day—30 December 2020—I was stopped by a gentleman, not a Jew, who asked me about the current political situation concerning Gibraltar's position on Brexit, which was only forty-eight hours away. I greeted him and told him, "Happy Christmas, my friend", referring to the Christmas that had just been celebrated only a few days earlier. He went on to say that Christmas was a pagan feast, that Jesus was a myth, and that he was a messianic believer. He opened his coat to show me the frills of a Jewish the 'prayer shawl' he was wearing.

He mentioned that it was Emperor Constantine who had introduced many pagan ideas into present day Christianity, something which was completely the opposite.

Christians in Constantine's era picked the time of the Roman feast of Saturnalia is correct but they replaced this with the Feast of Christmas since there was no biblical record that pinpointed the day in which Christ was born, unlike the crucifixation where there were notable days, so what the Christian Palestinians, Greeks and Romans did was, in fact do away with the pagan feast of Saturnalia, and thereby obliterated a pagan feast from the calendar for ever. Emperor Constantine was very wise.

The way in which Christmas was celebrate came much later in the days of Saint Francis, the green tree signified 'everlasting life' and the 'the stable, manger and animals the depiction of Christ's humble birth in a stable.

The person I spoke to was obviously well read and eloquent on the subject, and, was obviously clearly not alone in this thinking.

This exchange took place at the time when I was writing this booklet, with a Chapter on Heresies and it left me with food-for-thought.

I came to the conclusion that what this kind person was talking about was totally heretical. In a way it encouraged me to continue writing since I thought it would be timely.

I realized that there were people out there still seeking Jesus, and how fortunate it is that Christians have the privilege of knowing the Risen Christ, who promised and sent us the power of Pentecost to give us strength and show us the light.

Early Fathers Who Fought against Heresy

I am attempting to give the reader an idea of the immense difficulties that faced faithful Christians, not only during the early centuries, but also today, where people thirst for clarity and, therefore, the truth and challenged established religious beliefs and moral values.

The situation was becoming very serious from the early centuries to the middle ages. Several views or interpretations clashed with each other, and it became clear that someone had to take charge and control this great disparity within Christianity and moral values.

Variant Christian doctrines developed as Christianity grew, in the known world, by 40 per cent every ten years during the first and second centuries, even under persecution. The ante-Nicaea period saw a rise in the number of Christian sects, cults, and movements with strong characteristics but lacking in apostolic continuity. Different interpretations of scripture, particularly concerning the divinity of Christ birthed with two main heresies, Gnosticism and Arianism. One stating that Christ was Spiritual and had not died or been resurrected, and the other, that Christ was not divine.

The truth could only be determined from one source; it had to come from that branch of Christianity that could claim apostolic tradition!

Heresy is the formal denial of some truth of faith deemed by the teaching Church to be essential to the faith (dogma). Schism, which means to tear or rent, is the formal and wilful separation from the unity of the Church. Schism is not differences of opinions or interpretations of faith and doctrine, as is heresy, and therefore very difficult to debate. Schism is not opposed to faith but opposed to unity. In general, a schism has come about as a challenge to the central authority. For example, the Orthodox Catholic Church challenges the central authority of the Pope of the Apostolic Church in Rome.

The same early Fathers of the Church who condemned and fought these heresies, endowed with the Holy Spirit in the power of Pentecost, were responsible for the preservation and propagation of the Eucharist experience as a sacrifice and of the real presence as we know it today, as well as defining the true and full nature of Jesus, the Christ.

Some of these early Fathers were persecuted, exiled, and martyred. Their dedication in maintaining the apostolic beliefs should by itself suffice as to their authority and integrity.

Gnosticism

The name is derived from the Greek word "knowledge". They claimed that the function of Christ was to come as the emissary of the Supreme God, bringing "gnosis" (knowledge). They claimed that as a divine being, He did not assume a proper human body or died, but either temporarily inhabited a human, Jesus, or assumed a merely phantasmal human appearance. However, the Gospel of John starts, "And the Word was made flesh and lived amongst us" (John 1:1–18), so there is no question He was not human. But if Jesus was not human and did not die there would have been no resurrection and without resurrection there would be no 'salvation'.

Basically Gnosticism is a pre-Christian pagan concept full of fanciful mythology. It gave rise to many other splinter group heretical sects. One sect of Gnostics is the Manaeans, which has survived in Mesopotamia until present day.

Montanism

Montanism, an apocalyptic movement, developed in the latter half of the second century. It lived in expectation of the speedy outpouring of the Holy Spirit on the Church. They exalted themselves above the official hierarchy of the Church. It forbade second remarriage to the widowed and imposing it imposed vigorous fasting on everyone. It declared that the Holy Spirit had descended on Montanus. .

Arianism

Aranism was named after its founder, Arius, and formed circa 300.

This heresy denied the true divinity of Jesus Christ. It maintained that the Son of God was not eternal but created from nothing by the Father. Therefore, He was not God by nature.

Though fought by Athanasius and many other early bishops, this doctrine caused the greatest division in the Church between East and West. Several councils contradicted each other over this, and a series of exiles and counter-exiles ensued. The Church appeared totally Arian in philosophy and theology. St Jerome wrote, "The whole world groaned and marvelled to find itself Arian", though during those early centuries the various popes maintained faithfully to the doctrine of the early understanding of Christ's nature.

Athanasius, who was exiled, stuck to his guns. There was reconciliation and total rejection by all Western bishops against Aryanism.

Later, through a brilliant theological exposition of the Nicene faith or creed by three Cappadocians—St Basil, St Gregory of Nazianzus, and St Gregory of Nyssa—victory was finally achieved, after about sixty years of conflict, achieved in the Council of Constantinople in AD 381. It brought with it persecution of Catholics in North Africa and Spain. However by the year 500, Aryanism had finally disappeared.

There were also these: Apollonarianism, Subordinationism, Monophysitism, and Donatism. And *Sabellianism*, Formed in the early third century, Sabellianism believed that Father and Son were but different aspects or conditions of the one being. The three persons of the Holy Trinity were not realities or relations in the Godhead but merely relations of God to humankind

These are but a few of the numerous heresies which grew in the early centuries of the Christian Church and seriously divided at its roots. Providentially there were wise men that opposed and condemned these heresies which soon disappeared.

Liberation of Christian Worship

The liberation of Christianity was proclaimed by Emperor Constantine and meant that Christianity became fashionable and widespread through the Roman Empire, it was no longer persecuted. Communication within the Roman Empire was the best between territorial communities, but it was slow and cumbersome but nevertheless it spread.

It is important to bear in mind that as time went by, the Good News spread through the Empire against all odds, including mass executions, until the great Roman Emperor Constantine, who had converted to Christianity and thereby changed the Roman Empire from persecutors of Christ to Christians. Once the Emperor became a Christian, it became fashionable for his subjects also to become Christians.

At the same time Constantine changed the location of the capital of the empire from Rome to *Nova Roma*. That city was later named Constantinople-- after Emperor Constantine. By moving the capital away from Rome, he disassociated the capital of Christianity from the latent pagan tradition of ancient Rome to a city free from idolatry and full of Christian churches. In Nova Roma there were neither arenas of violence nor statues to pagan emperors. Christianity was taught in the many new churches that were built in Constantinople and the rest of the Empire.

Constantine's decision to cease the persecution of Christians in the Roman Empire was a turning point for the rapid spreading of Christianity, sometimes referred to as the Triumph of the Church, the Peace of the Church, or the Constantinian Shift.

In 313 Constantine and Licinius issued the Edict of Milan, decriminalizing Christian worship. Christian worship was now legal!

The Emperor became a great patron of the Church and set a precedent for the position of "Christian Emperor." He raised the notion of orthodoxy with ecumenical councils and the state church of the Roman Empire, declaring this by edict in 380.

In the Eastern Orthodox Church, Oriental Orthodox Church, and various Eastern Catholic Churches, Constantine is revered as a saint and *isapostolos* for his example as a Christian monarch.

Constantine's mother, Helena, had been a Christian long before Constantine converted. She travelled to the Holy Land and was instrumental in locating or identifying the many locations of the holy sites where Jesus had been, such as the Holy Sepulchre and Golgotha, the place of the crucifixion, and Bethlehem.

Helena built, with her son's blessing, plenty of commemorative churches in all these locations. She is said, not confirmed, to have discovered the remnant of the Holy Cross and the lance with which Longinus pierced Jesus' side.

The excellent organization of the Roman Empire at the time, its road system, and its communication system helped in the propagation and expansion of the Christian faith. The Holy Spirit continued to guide the spreading of the gospel.

One clear instance which also infused the spread of the Word was when St Jerome (312–420) undertook a similar task as St Luke. Of all the things that made Jerome famous, since nothing was as legendary as his translation of the scriptures from the Greek and Aramaic, into Latin, the common and official language throughout the Roman Empire.

With the prompting of Pope Damascus, Jerome began this monumental piece of work while he was still in Rome. He spent his entire life translating the scriptures. He translated—from the earliest known manuscripts available, the Old Testament and the New Testament books, the first group from the Hebrew language and the second group from Greek manuscripts—into Latin.

Jerome was inclined to the monastic life and started the monastic Order of St Jerome, based in Bethlehem. It was where he was buried, though his remains were later moved to Rome.

He was an extremely learned person, a tireless writer on many topics, and in the process and with care; he sorted between the great variety of documents both apostolic and apocryphal. The former was the recognized authentic scriptures that conformed to the faith of early believers and their thinking. The latter was from those which were considered not to follow the apostolic faith and tradition of the early Fathers of the Christian Church. Such an exercise was required of the highest level of analysis and discernment between apostolic and non-apostolic beliefs. Over the centuries his work has stood the scrutiny of critical modern scripture scholars.

His selection of original documents formed the first Codex of the first complete Christian Bible readable throughout the Empire. This Bible became known as the *Vulgate Bible,* "vulgate" because it was in the official and common language of the Roman Empire, Latin. Each Bible had to be handwritten so that mass production did not come about until the printing process invention by Johannes Gutenberg.

The following known phrases are attributable to St Jerome:

The face is the mirror of the mind, and eyes, without speaking, confess the secrets of the heart.

Good, better, best. Never let it rest, till your good is better and your better is best.

True friendship ought never to conceal what it thinks.

He was recognized as one of the greatest doctors of the church, together with St Augustine of Hippo (354–430). In fact, the two were contemporaries and corresponded, forming a distant but close relationship.

Is not the above list of heresies enough to send people crazy and give up? Yes, but luckily there were many other who stood by the faith.

The Struggle and Solution of the Apostolic Church

It was the Power of Pentecost that gave wisdom to early Christian to direct the Church in the Faith.

We can imagine the great confusion that must have plagued those attempting to keep the Church on the right track. As we will see, the infant church encountered all these challenges concerning the plurality of beliefs. So it became necessary for the church fathers to define a profession of faith which upheld all the important orthodox and apostolic beliefs by which a Christian would acknowledge to be truly a follower of Christ Jesus.

They summarized their faith by proclaiming a creed, a profession of faith. This creed formula was established at the Council of Nicea in 325, and subsequently ratified and endorsed by the Council of Constantinople in 381 plus other important councils. The Council of Nicea became an ecumenical council that dealt with the many other questions and heresies plaguing the Church. Constantine was responsible for encouraging the Council of Nicea, the first ecumenical council

Constantine also helped the Church financially and built numerous basilicas. He was also responsible for the restoration of several holy sites in the Holy Land, such as the Church of the Holy Sepulchre and the church at Bethlehem.

In 316 he acted as judge in North Africa in the first ecumenical Council there concerning the Donatist controversy which was eventually squashed. After the Council of Nicea decreed a decision on Christ's divinity, he enforced the doctrine. He rooted out heresies and upheld ecclesiastical unity.

The last and most severe persecution organized against Christianity was authorized Emperor Diocletian, 303–311. The Creed formula itself underwent incredible challenges and controversy. It was repudiated and discarded for several decades by powerful factions, both temporal and spiritual. Finally, it was restored through the tenacious and eloquent exposition and arguments by St Athanasius and later by St Basil and the two St Gregory's.

The Creed upheld the recognition of one God, the Holy Trinity, and Jesus' nature of, "begotten, not made", the place of the Holy Spirit as part of the same Godhead, the Apostolic and universality (Katolicus) of Christ's Church, and the Immaculate Conception of Mary.

Interestingly, in defining Jesus' nature and divinity as God-made man, the councils and scholars could not avoid exploring Mary's position and the part she played in God's plan of salvation. The question was, if Jesus was God-made man, who was Mary in this relationship? The issue of *Theotokos*, the mother of God, or the "Mother of Him who was God", not begotten but of the incarnate God through the Holy Spirit (which are inseparable), came about because of the question about who was Christ?

This gave rise to the honour that the Apostolic Church gives to Mary. It was an obvious and logical revelation which was arrived at once. As the mother of God, she must have been conceived without sin since sin cannot abide where God abides. Jesus' own humanness and divinity were defined.

Why is this creed relevant to our narrative on the Eucharist? Simply this, that the same people who had been guided by the Holy Spirit, who had upheld this Truth, also upheld the Faith on the

Real Presence' as well as the Sacrificial nature of the Eucharist, particularly presently by the Catholic and Eastern Orthodox Mass.

Many powerful men suffered when they opposed a strongly established heresy, such as Aryanism. These were St Athanasius, St Basil, and the two Gregory's. Providentially, these apostolic bishops and scholars challenged those erroneous biblical interpretations and called them heresies. These men, who we will meet later, argued forcefully against these errors with biblical arguments. Guided by the Holy Spirit, these heresies were defeated one by one. As readers will soon appreciate, it took great wisdom and fidelity to the truth of the Gospels to fight and defeat all the above heresies.

Again providentially, these records have survived to this day.

Apostolic Fathers of the Church

Only the Power of Pentecost gave early Christians the strength to fight against heresies.

We have read a brief summary of the main early heresies which were complicated theological and mythical interpretations of the life, person, and mission of Jesus Christ. These erroneous interpretations were formulated into doctrines by well-meaning religious people, intellectuals, and politicians. Many of them were bishops, preachers of Christianity. There is no doubt that these people sincerely believed in what they said and did. This became their kind of faith.

The Christian notion of belief became more concrete as the Church gradually developed in the face of opposition. Faith became a mystery imparted to Christians (1 Tim. 3:9) and is something to be preserved (2 Tim. 4:7; Rev. 14:12).

These were the golden rules then applied by the early Fathers when fighting errors. These Herculean controversies produced growth in understanding of the Faith and obliquely produced renewal and reform with every challenge, but never departing from the basic truth!

The phrase "Fathers of the Church" embraces all ancient Christian writers down to Gregory the Great (d 636) in the West, and John of Damascus (d 749) in the East.

The earliest writers, the Apostolic Fathers, identified faith with the acceptance of the Christian message. As the young Church progressively detached itself from normative Judaism and entered the mainstream of Greek-Roman civilization, it confronted the challenge of communicating the message of Jesus across diverse social, intellectual, and cultural lines. This task fell in the beginning on the Apostolic Fathers (pupils of the Apostles), who became the Apologists that defended the Apostolic faith.

These defenders of the Faith through their faith, and guided by the Holy Spirit, preached throughout their regions, and their letters were circulated throughout the Christian world. Their preaching and letters, though not canonical, are as lucid and pastoral as were the letters of Peter, James, and Paul. The faithful communities looked forward thirstily for their teachings.

Most of these writings are kept in the ancient archives in the Vatican. We owe the preservation of our present Faith to their apostolic tradition and seal.

It must have been the Power of Pentecost that illuminated these Apostolic Fathers of the early Church.

The following is a list of these great personalities.

Clement of Rome—Bishop of Rome, Martyr (d 100). Who wrote to the Corinthians, "Do we not have one God and one Christ and one Spirit of grace, a Spirit poured out upon us?"

Ignatius of Antioch—Bishop of Antioch, Martyr (d 107). Wrote numerous epistles.

Hermas c. 140. Herma was a prophet and visionary. He wrote the famous *The Shepherd*. He is referred to by many early Fathers.

Polycarp—Bishop of Smyrna, Martyr (c. 69–155). Polycarp was a leading Christian figure in Roman Asia. A staunch defender of orthodoxy, he combated the heretics Narcionites and Valentinians.

Papias—Bishop of Hierappolis in Asia (c. 60–130). He was a disciple of "John" and companion of Polycarp. Wrote "Expositions of the Oracles of the Lord". It is he who writes that Mark was the interpreter of St Peter the Elder.

Fathers of the Church

The Fathers of the Church were characterized by orthodoxy of doctrine, holiness of life, and approval of the church and antiquity.

Justin—Martyr (c. 100–165).

A great apologist. Wrote the "First Apology" to Emperor Antoninus Pius and his sons; "Dialogue with Trypho", a Jew; and the "Second Apology", addressed to the Roman Senate.

Irenaeus—Bishop of Lyons (130–200). Great theologian. Wrote "Against Heresies", and attacks against Gnosticism, Montanism, and Valentinians. He argued based purely on scriptural arguments.

St Hippolytus—Martyr (170–236). An important third-century theologian. For a while in a schism with Rome, but though he had differences with Rome, before his death he reconciled with Rome. His body was brought to Rome for burial. His main work was "Refutation of Heresies" and "Apostolic Tradition" among many others.

The Didache

Didache literally meant "teaching", composed about 100. It explains how Christians lived and what they believed and practised. A sort of guide or manual for early Christians. Contains instructions on baptism, fasting, prayer, the Eucharist, and how to treat prophets, bishops, and deacons.

St Clement of Alexandria—Martyr (150–215).

Though he held to a soft form of Gnosis, he contributed great theological works. His greatest was "Paedagogus", on Christian life and manners, and his "Quis Dives Salvetus?" an exposition on Mark 10:17–31.

Tertullian (c. 160–225).

A prolific Christian writer, he adopted Montanism of a sort. But all his other works based fundamentally on scripture were sufficient to justify the title of "Father of Latin Theology".

He argued against Gnostics, Spiritualism, Hermogenes, Valentinians, and Marcion with devastating power based on scripture.

Oirgen—(185–254).

Biblical critic, exegete, theologian, and spiritual writer. A fertile author. His thoughts were nourished on scripture. His father was martyred in Alexandria. He suffered constant persecution. Great defence against the Marcianites.

The following is a list of the continuing Fathers of the Church. A short account of their lives may be found in the *British Encyclopaedia* or at *Wikipedia* on the internet.

St Basil—329–379. - *St Augustine*—354–430. - *Cyril of Jerusalem*—Bishop of Jerusalem (c. 386), Fought against Aryanism and wrote the twenty-four Catechesis. - *St Athanasius*—d. 373. - *St John of Damascus*—304–384. Elected pope. Fought against Aryanism, Donatism, Macedonianism, and Luciferians. It was he who commissioned St Jerome to revise the Bible and draw up the Canon of Scriptural Books, which he promulgated.

St Martin of Tours—371. Bishop of Tours, evangelist. - *St Patrick*—389–461. Evangelist and missionary. - *St John Chrysostom*—d 407. Evangelist, lawyer, doctor of the church. Persecuted unlawfully by the empress and church rivals. - *St Jerome*—d 420. Biblical scholar, evangelist, theologian. *St Columbanus*—c. 543–615 Missionary in England, France, and Italy. *St Gregory the Great*—d 636. Became pope. Writer, preacher, reformer. Reintroduced music into the liturgy. Strong yet humble. By popular acclamation he was canonized immediately after his death.

Isidore of Spain—Bishop of Seville d 636. He fought against Aryanism. He was an evangelist and founder of schools. Famous as a scholar for his prolific writings, for his sanctity, and for helping the poor. Defender of the faith against barbarians.

Readers are advised to bear in mind that the above persons are but a few of the principal personalities involved in the defence of the Apostolic Faith, people who were learned preachers and teachers, Disciples, and followers of Jesus Christ and the apostolic heritage who defended the faith that had been handed to them by Jesus Himself.

The Nicene Creed

The Nicene Creed'

It was thanks to the guidance that came from the Power of Pentecost that this Council established the Cannon of Faith. Known as the Nicene Creed.

The Christian profession of Faith established at the Council of Nicea in AD 325.][defined the term of, "Homoousios", a Greek Christian theological term, describing Jesus as, "same in being", or, "same in essence", with God the Father. The same term was later applied to the Holy Spirit in order to designate Him as being, "same in essence", with the Father and the Son.

THE NICENE CREED.

We believe in one God,
   the Father, the Almighty,
   maker of heaven and earth,
   and of all that is, seen and unseen.

We believe in one Lord, Jesus Christ,
   the only Son of God,
   eternally begotten of the Father,
   God from God, Light from Light,
   true God from true God,
   begotten, not made, one in Being with the Father.
   Through him all things were made.
   For us men and for our salvation,
      he came down from heaven:
by the power of the Holy Spirit
he was born of the Virgin Mary, and became man.

For our sake he was crucified under Pontius Pilate;
   he suffered, died, and was buried.
   On the third day he rose again
      in fulfilment of the Scriptures;
   he ascended into heaven
      and is seated at the right hand of
      the Father.
He will come again in glory to judge
      the living and the dead,
   and his kingdom will have no end.

We believe in the Holy Spirit,
   the Lord, the giver of life,
   who proceeds from the Father and the Son.
With the Father and the Son he
   is worshipped and glorified.
He has spoken through the Prophets.
We believe in one holy catholic
   and apostolic Church.
We acknowledge one baptism
   for the forgiveness of sins.
We look for the resurrection of the dead,
   and the life of the world to come.
   Amen.

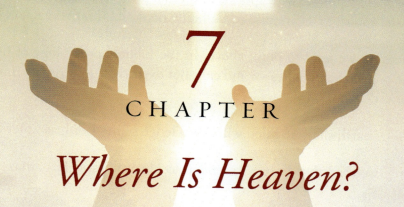

7
CHAPTER

Where Is Heaven?

My life story, and yours, and where we find ourselves today are a beautiful piece of God's work in us, despite our shortcomings, mistakes. That is why I believe that everything cannot end with death. All that wondrous life-time work of every soul who have lived in this world cannot disappear into thin air or ashes. There must be, surely a purpose for life.

If you happen to be a person of faith and believe in the All Mighty irrespective of religion—Zen, Muslim, Jewish, or Christian—or even someone from the darkest or remote region in the furthest corner of a jungle or desert, for some incredible reason we find that people have through the ages believed in a Higher Power, compelling them to worship, invoking it in prayer for protection, or imploring for a plentiful harvest.

The Egyptians, for example, believed in an afterlife and even provided for the journey of that soul to some afterlife destination, possibly what they considered to be heaven.

The Vikings also had no deity and were fierce pagans. They placed their dead in a cremation vessel, or funeral pyre that prepared the dead for their last journeys. They filled the vessel with the deceased's belongings so that they would enjoy a long and happy afterlife with all the trappings they owned in their former lives.

The funeral pyre was specifically set with special wood that produced lots of smoke which was meant to help carry the deceased's spirit to its afterlife in Valhalla, no doubt their concept of heaven.

When we refer to heaven, we tend to point above. In the biblical cosmology of heaven, heaven is the arena of God and the angels that touches on and calls out to earth, the arena of humans, animals, plants, and planets.

Isaiah anticipated, "The earth shall be filled with knowledge of the Lord, as water covers the seas."

In a Christian setting, we read that Jesus, "Ascended to Heaven", and His amazed Disciples saw him travel upwards.

Elijah the prophet also went up to heaven:

> "You have asked a difficult thing", Elijah said, "yet if you see me when I am taken from you, it will be yours—otherwise not." As they were walking along and talking together, suddenly a chariot and horses of fire appeared and separated the two of them, and Elijah went up to heaven in a whirlwind. (2 King 2–11)

Jesus is quoted as saying that "In my Father's house there are many mansions." Where are these mansions? In Hebrews 1–3, Paul writes, "When he had cleansed us from our sins, he sat down at the right hand of the Majesty in heaven."

Heaven, in many religions, is the abode of God as well as of angels, deified humans, the blessed dead, and other celestial beings. It is often conceived as an expanse that overarches the earth, stretching overhead like a canopy, dome, or vault and encompassing the sky and upper atmosphere; the sun, moon, and stars; and the transcendent realm beyond.

The psalmist says, "From Heaven the Lord looks down and sees all mankind. From his fixed throne he beholds all who dwell on the earth" (Ps. 33:13–14). "The Lord looks down..." Here Heaven is above.

In Psalm 23, the psalmist ends his prayer with, "You anoint my head with oil; my cup overflows. Only goodness and kindness follow me all the days of my life; I will live in the house of the Lord forever." A pious aspiration to God's house, a place in heaven?

In most cultures, heaven is synonymous with order.

Every reference to heaven points up.

If we stand at the North Pole, heaven is above. But if we stand at the South Pole, heaven is still above, but on the opposite sides to the North Pole. The fact is that the starry sky and the cosmos are all around us—North, South, East, and West. An infinite space of stars but every one of these points is above...

On clear starry nights I have often looked up to the sky and marvelled at the immense expanse of the stars that glow from above. According to scientists this infinite layer of stars goes on and on and on to an extent that even with the most powerful telescope, has not been able to fathom. Astronomers recently discovered that there are galaxies through the far reaches of the black holes.

I have wondered if this apparently infinite and impenetrable universe is the space where heaven spans to provide the many mansions that the Father has in His house. The 'House' need not be a house of bricks and mortar, but God's domain.

On the other hand, I have always understood that heaven is not necessarily a physical place but a state of being.

This state of being could be what we call heaven and being in God's presence or domain.

However these are only my own thoughts. But then there is another imponderable. The Christian Faith asserts to the resurrection of the dead and life everlasting. Where will the heavenly setting be so as to cater for so many billions after this 'resurrection'?

To answer this question, there is a beautiful biblical quotation that should fill us with hope:

> *Then I saw new heavens and a new earth. The former heavens and the former earth had passed away, and the sea was no longer.*

I saw a New Jerusalem, the holy city, coming down out of heaven from God, beautiful as a bride prepared to meet her husband. I heard a voice coming from the throne cry out: "This is God's dwelling among men. He shall dwell with them and they shall be his people and he shall be their God who is always with them. He shall wipe every tear from their eyes, and there shall be no more death or mourning, crying out or pain, for the former world has passed away."

"The One who sat on the throne said to me, "See, I make all things new!" (Rev. 21:1–12)

I refuse to accept that death is the end of life, that all that was lived was for nothing, that the love that my mother and father gave me has gone forever. That my brother's dedication was for nothing, that my sister's unselfish years of sacrifice helping the poor, that St. Damian's and St. Teresa's of Calcutta and thousands of missionaries around the world, was just wasted time, senseless and empty pious was for nothing?

No, sir, this would be totally illogical. Life would then have been meaningless. The promise of Eternal life makes more sense.

Maranatha, Come Lord Jesus.

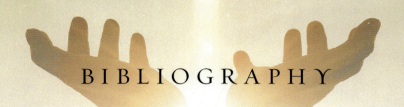

BIBLIOGRAPHY

NEW AMERICAN BIBLE – 1970/76

The Churches the Apostles Left Behind. -----Fr. Raymond Brown S.S.

The Gospel according to John. Ditto.

A Once -- Coming of the Holy Spirit ---------- Ditto .

A New Pentecost. Leon Joseph Suenens. Cardinal.

Ecumenism and Charismatic Renewal. Ditto

Baptism in the Holy Spirit Ditto.

Jerome's Bible Commentaries. ----By: Raymond E. Brown S.S., Joseph A Fitzmeyer, S.J., Roland E. Murphy.

SUGGESTIONS FOR FURTHER READING

The Jerome Biblical Commentary - Edited by R.E. Brown, J .A. Fitzmyers, S.J., and R.E. Murphy.

A First Century Chalice Dispute - Kilmartin, S.J. The Early Christian Fathers- H. Bettenson- Oxford University Press

Catholic and Christian- Dr. Allan Scheck

St. of the Day, Vole, 1 & 2- L. Foley O.F.M. - St. Anthony Messenger Press

The Churches the Apostles Left Behind - R.E. Brown, S.S. Paulist Press

The Gospel According to John - R.E.Brown, S.S. Catholicism- R.P. McBrien, Winston Press

Preaching the Lectionary - R.H. Fuller, the Liturgical Press

New Testament Words- W. Barclay

The Gospel of John - W. Barclay'

'Stones' Complete Concordance

Scripture Discussion Commentary of Paul- Vol. 1 & 11. L. Bright et al - Sheed & Ward

The Power of Praise and Worship- T. Law, Victory House

Publication

Your Spiritual Weapons- T. Law, Victory House

The Oxford Dictionary of the Christian Church - Cross & Livingston, Oxford University Press

The Bible: New American

Vatican Council II, Vol. I and II, Austin Flannery, O.P.

A Catechism of the Catholic Church - R.J. Fox, Franciscan Herald Press

The Bread of Life- David E. Rosage, Servant Books

Charism and Charismatic Renewal- Francis A. Sullivan S.J. Servant Books

Jesus the New Elijah- Paul Hiddenbauch, O.P.

History and Theology in the Fourth Gospel - J. Louis Martyn, Abingdon, Nashville

Anglican-Roman Catholic International Commission- The Final Report, 1981

Evangelic Nuntiandi- Pope Paul VI- 1971

Antiquities- Flavious Josephus

ABOUT THE AUTHOR

Joe L Caruana, MBE; GMD, is a poly-faceted man.

H.M Queen Elizabeth II awarded Joe with the MBE, (Member of the British Empire) for 25 years of altruistic work addicts and for starting the first Rehabilitation Centre for Gibraltar. The second award, GMD, (Gibraltar Medal of Distinction) was for his services as Minister in the Gibraltar Government from 1969, when the Land Frontier with Spain was closed by the Dictator Franco, when Joe was blacklisted as 'Persona non Grata' in Spain.

His list of six books includes *Spirit of the Phoenician*, his own 'autobiography', setting his Maltese's family history his then Second book, *When the Hangman Came*, an intriguing true murder story in a building where Joe's grandparents lived. *The Iron Knight of Malta*, a historical novel on about Grand Master of the Order of St. John of Jerusalem, Jean de la Valette, in 1565 when he successfully withstood the Ottoman, against overwhelming odds and saved the rest of Europe from Muslim rule. *Eyes Set on Heaven* is the biography of Joe's brother the saintly Bishop Charles Caruana. ***The Life and Times of Sir Robert Peliza***, Joe's fifth book the biography of Joe's former charismatic political leader and, Chief Minister of Gibraltar.

Started work as a junior draughtsman, then as technical representative, then gaming casino pit-boss, entrepreneur owning two retail shops and a wholesale business of frozen fish. Simultaneously he entered politics and held the posts of Minister for Health also Public Works.

He immigrated to Canada and, together with two partners, started a diamond coring company and two manufacturing factories of industrial diamond drilling bits for the Oil and Gas Industry. He was an Honorary Member of the Professional Engineers' Club.

Joe was born in Gibraltar 1937. When WWII started Joe and his family were evacuated to French Morocco, when France fell the Germans took control of Morocco and Joe and his family were evacuated to London. In the UK they experienced the devastating German Blitz, the worst period in UK's history. After four years there with their place of residence receiving a direct hit by a German V1- guided bomb, the family was re-evacuated to Ballymena, Northern Island living in isolated country-side in improvised Military Nissen Huts. They lived there for 4 years in severe cold and shortage of food and clothing, with no formal schooling.

Now in the sunset of his life, as a legacy to his Christian faith, which he says emanates from the days when St Paul's was shipwrecked on the Island of Malta.

He wishes to share his spiritual journey, *The Power of the Pentecost, The Power in Hands, so that he present generation is aware of the many difficulties, persecutions and religious divisions, the Apostolic Churches and Christian Faith continues to undergo in recent days.*

Printed in the United States
by Baker & Taylor Publishing Services

Printed in the United States
by Baker & Taylor Publisher Services